Heartworm Survival Guide

Every Pet Owner's Guide to Understanding, Preventing and Treating Heartworm Disease

Joseph Bottone

Heartwormsurvivalguide.com

Petroglyph Publishing

This book is not intended as a substitute for the medical advice of a veterinarian but is only intended for the education and entertainment of the reader. The reader should regularly consult a veterinarian in matters relating to his/her pet's health and particularly with respect to any symptoms that may require diagnosis or medical attention. Individual readers are solely responsible for their own decisions related to their pet's health. The author and the publisher does not accept responsibility for any adverse effects individuals may claim that their pet's experience, whether directly or indirectly, from the information contained in this book.

Even though particular organizations, websites and products are mentioned in this book, that does not mean that the author or publisher endorse any of the information they provide or recommendations they may make.

HEARTWORM SURVIVAL GUIDE: EVERY PET OWNER'S GUIDE TO UNDERSTANDING, PREVENTING AND TREATING HEARTWORM DISEASE. FIRST EDITION

PUBLISHED BY PETROGLYPH PUBLISHING

HEARTWORMSURVIVALGUIDE.COM

ISBN-13: 978-0-615-82830-5

7 6 5 4 3 2 1

For Lucy & Molly

Contents

Foreword

Heartworm disease continues to destroy the health of our pets despite a growing awareness of the parasite. Heartworm infections are increasing both locally and globally as well. There was never a time more important for a book to shed some light on the heartworm problem than now.

Anyone that has witnessed the effects of the disease first hand knows the insidious damage the heartworms can cause. No pets or their owners should ever have to go through that.

Unfortunately, many people inside and out of animal medicine have many false beliefs and assumptions about the heartworm. It could be said that we are still in the dark ages of understanding the disease.

Fortunately, you have opened this book to find some real answers. Perhaps you have a pet that was recently diagnosed as being heartworm positive. Never before has it been so important to educate yourself on the subject. Or, you might just want to make sure that you provide the best possible care for your precious and beloved pet. This book might also be given away as a gift to someone who would benefit.

As you read through this book any anxiety you have about the issue will lessen and you will find yourself more empowered to make intelligent choices for your pets. This book was designed as a guide to help and comfort you while your animals are protected and healed.

Also, as you read the following pages, please keep in mind that this book was not written to convince you of any opinion. Instead, it is intended to simply educate in the best possible way so that you can make the right choice at the right time.

One

Down the Wormhole

I WAS ONLY AWARE OF THE TERM heartworm from hearsay, just like most dog owners. Each time my dogs and I found ourselves at the veterinarian's office, I could not help but notice the posters all over the walls plastered with dire warnings and horrific pictures and illustrations. There were many images of worms and blood, and if it was not for that glass jar full of formaldehyde and a severed heart infected with worms, I might have missed the message. Oh yes, heartworm is serious business: a multi billion dollar industry!

On a rainy afternoon, I was given the sign by my two black labs that they wanted to go on a walk by the river. And their wagging tails, whines and bulging eyes got us out the door quickly. The walk was beautiful and graced with huge cottonwood trees, soft dirt for our feet, and a body of water for my dogs to play and cool off in. They were full of boundless energy that day, and I remember forging ahead where we normally would turn back. The memory of that decision to go forward is very clear in my mind; it changed the course of my life in a major and permanent way. Looking back on it I am amazed how we are sometimes guided by very small events which open a door we never dreamed we would walk through.

That "very small thing" was, in this case, a porcupine. My dog Lucy was as usual, leading the parade. She often keeps ahead of us by 20 feet or more while my other dog Molly guards the rear. I began to feel a little anxious as we walked deeper into the woods and into a mass of bushes that the trail winded through. The atmosphere all around became darker and as I felt the cold evading my body I immediately saw my dog Lucy leap into the bushes and disappear followed seconds later by my other dog, Molly.

Waiting for a few moments alone on the trail, I listened for sounds that would convey some information about my dog's whereabouts. Them galloping off at full throttle towards some even faster critter was nothing new. But this time I was alarmed at the sound of a yelp coming from somewhere within the bush. I was worried and started calling their names to come back, but waited in silence. To my great astonishment, Lucy suddenly appeared on my side of the bush with a nose full of porcupine quills! I will never forget that look on her face, a comical mix of surprise and wonder at the creature that outwitted her. Next, came Molly out of the bushes with twice the number of quills but the same silly expression.

My first reaction to seeing them was to laugh. I told them that we have to turn around and get back to the car and out of this crazy mess that we stumbled into. I felt like I should have turned around when I started to feel uneasy. I pulled a couple loose quills out of their noses which now resembled the hairy and spiky porcupine himself. I could see in their eyes the memory of the porcupine fading quickly and to confirm this they trotted off and were ready for the next adventure.

We arrived home later that night and immediately began to formulate a plan to remove the quills. There was not more than a couple quarters to rub together in the bank at the time so I tried to avoid the vet's office. Utilizing a "do it yourself" kit composed of a pair of heavy duty pliers and a coffee can to put the quills into, I hunkered down to do the job that none of us looked forward to.

What followed was a blur of hours spent chasing down each dog one at a time to at least try to catch a quill into the teeth of the pliers. This was near impossible however and I realized the enormous strength that they possessed. But eventually the quills came out one by one until I had at least 20 or so clanking in the bottom of the can. But alas, there were some quills that however hard I tried to remove, were too deeply buried inside their now aching lips.

"Looking back on it I am amazed how we are sometimes guided by very small events which open a door we never dreamed we would walk through."

Exhausted and ready to call it a day, we fell asleep trying to forget about having to go the veterinarian's office in the morning.

On waking the memory of the porcupine and his quills came rushing back like the remembrance of something purposely misplaced. When we arrived at the veterinarian's office my dogs were greeted with sighs of "poor babies" by the assistants waiting by the desk. After signing in we sat down and waited for the relief that was to come.

Unfortunately, the relief of removing the porcupine quills came with the price of an outstandingly large medical bill. But before being served the check, my eyes happened to glance on one of those posters that mesmerize all who try to evade its menacing glare. So in a typical fashion I asked the veterinarian how expensive a heartworm test would cost. Trying to conceal my dropping jaw I asked how accurate the tests were and was reprimanded with the answer that they were very accurate. Later, both my dogs were given a heartworm test which I would later find out would need a second series of tests and more money for a "confirmation."

DOWN THE WORMHOLE

About a week later I was awakened by a call by the veterinarian and was told that my dog Lucy tested positive for heartworms and that we would need to come in for another test. I was alarmed and upset at this news as most people would be. But only because, I came to later understand, I was led to believe that the nature of the heartworm was incurable with any other means except with some dangerous and expensive drug. This is the gleaming point in time that we slid down into a long and winding tunnel of hearsay and contradictory bits of information. I found myself wanting to help Lucy as quickly as possible but felt paralyzed being naturally very suspicious of the major pharmaceutical behemoths.

Some of the information that the veterinarian told me over the telephone I immediately knew were broken puzzle pieces and did not represent the whole at all. I realized with intuition that what she was telling me was only being replayed to me, it was something that she recorded like a tape in her mind from hearing endless hours of rhetoric. Every book, teacher, peer and reference she was influenced by drilled it into her mind that their answer for the heartworm was gospel and undisputed. Though I know that most veterinarians have a dog's best interest at heart and mean well, I also realize that most can only offer the help that they themselves have been given.

One of the most obvious misguided insights the veterinarian told me was that the heartworm that Lucy tested positive for was fatal within at least three years and that there was only one cure in the entire world for this ancient and natural disease. That the only cure on the face of God's planet is a poison; the only drug that is FDA approved in the United States for the treatment of heartworm is manufactured by Merial called Immiticide®.

I remember feeling angry when the veterinarian told me that this drug was so strong that it could kill my dog. She explained that some dogs are not strong enough for the force of the drug. Later, I also learned that since the drug kills adult worms so quickly, an embolism could develop from the dead worms getting blocked in the arteries. The veterinarian told me that I would have to keep Lucy quiet and not let her run or get any exercise for three months! All the while her mouth was reciting these things my mind started flashing red lights and turning on the sirens. The fact that this drug could kill my dog made me group it into the same category as the heartworm and label it a threat. And I instinctively knew that trying to keep Lucy from exercise would not only prove to be impossible (both her and Molly love chasing anything that moves) but also be depressing to her overall mood.

I imagine that anyone who needs to inject their dog with a toxic drug designed in a lab by a company that has been profiting on our sicknesses for too long would feel some level of doubt. And I kept wondering why did my vet assume that Lucy would need this drug in the first place before going over more options with me? I came to believe that you can follow a money trail which would reveal true motivations. Indeed, the treatment would be very expensive, almost out of my reach financially and might kill my dog.

WHICH WAY IS UP?

After the conversation with the veterinarian, and immediately after slipping the phone back onto its cradle, I felt depressed. The feeling of being told your dog has heartworm (but needs more expensive tests just to be sure) without understanding anything about the parasite, was an increasing panic. The longer I let the news about the heartworm sink in, the more I felt helpless. And the longer that I felt helpless, the more confused I became.

A feeling similar to being lost in some strange and ominous woods would be common to people just finding out that their pet has heartworm. This is when centering your attention on finding some honest answers will provide some relief.

I began researching in books, medical journals and online for answers. I had no idea that I would be opening a can of worms that would fuel more than a thousand hours of research as I unearthed one mystery after another. The pinnacle of achievement cumulated into the book you are reading right now, and the healing and resolution of Lucy's heartworm "problem."

The fact that heartworm is complicated cannot be understated. Heresy gets passed around until it becomes what people mistake as the truth. You not only see this in the information people share with one another, but in academic literature as well. There is simply not enough research by people who are not profit driven.

Locating and discerning correct information about heartworm is like unraveling a ball of tangled yarn. But I found out that the problem of heartworm is much less complicated than it is claimed to be. So forget everything you have heard about before.

The Reason for the Season

This book's only purpose is to make you feel less bewildered and more empowered to treat your dog, cat or ferret in the best possible way. By reading this, you are taking your own very capable ability to make informed and intelligent choices for your pet into your own hands.

It was a good thing that I was suspicious about what the veterinarian told me. Amazingly, she never mentioned anything

---

> "I imagine that anyone who needs to inject their dog with a toxic drug designed in a lab by a company that has been profiting on our sicknesses for too long would feel some level of doubt."

---

about new and safer treatments for heartworm disease. I am also glad that I was initially skeptical and leery regarding the "authority" of the veterinarian. We are not living in the dark ages anymore, yet some veterinarians still practice outdated heartworm treatments.

The information about the best way to treat animals for heartworm is fiercely guarded by the ones who want to control you, the pet owner, for reasons of profit. By withholding this information from you it hopes to make you powerless and under control by those who think they "know best."

All this only causes unneeded suffering by the living population of Earth. For example, the company Merial who manufactures the only current drug approved by the FDA to treat heartworm disease ran out of the drug in 2009. As a result, many animal shelters around the world began to euthanize dogs and cats that came in with heartworms, only because of the erroneous idea that without that particular drug heartworms were untreatable. Situations like that can be avoided by putting this knowledge into everyone's hands. By sifting through the information, we will present to you the most accurate knowledge about treating heartworm disease.

This book addresses you, the reader, at your level of need. There will be some of you that have been given a positive result for your pet's heartworm test. This book will hold your hand and comfort you by lessening your fears and anxiety surrounding it all. You will be led through the assembly of those that have mixed agendas and intentions for you and your pet, and into the light of genuine information. This includes the safest and best way to treat your animals in all circumstances.

Cost is a real concern for many people. Unfortunately, many people have a discriminatory attitude to those whose budgets might be a little tight regarding their pets. Although it is important for animals to be well taken care of, someone might think twice about adopting an animal if they do not believe they can provide the same care that those who buy organic and grass fed meat for their dogs do. That animal might never get taken home to a loving family just because of a person's concern of what other people might think. But an animal that receives copious amounts of love will always thrive.

Unfortunately, heartworm preventatives and treatment can be expensive. This might cause some people to forgo these for their pets. For those readers who are concerned about the costs surrounding heartworm please understand this: the best possible preventative and treatment for heartworm can be done for pennies instead of hundreds of dollars if some simple knowledge is understood. Information is powerful, and the most current and highest form of treatment can be given to your pets very inexpensively. This is clearly explained to you in a later chapter.

The principal purpose of this book is to eliminate as much as possible the space between you and the healing and preventing of disease in your pet. If you were to seek this from a veterinarian you might have to listen to a high pressure sales pitch about all the expensive drugs you will need to buy to help your animal. You might feel bullied as they prey on your emotions and try to make you feel guilty and like a bad pet owner. I am sure most veterinarians have the best intentions, yet the fact remains that they might do this anyway. However, since cost is no longer a concern, you can make your own decisions.

You can also use this information to work alongside your veterinarian to come up with the best treatment for your pet. Or you can go it alone, and find what works best for you. There is simply too many variables in each animal's health status to recommend one solution to the heartworm problem. Therefore, I will not push my opinion for treatment onto you. The best I can do is offer you the facts, and let you take those into consideration as you move forward.

I know that by reading this book you will be empowered to help your pets live a longer and more vibrant life. I wrote this book for every animal that could suffer from heartworm disease, and for their guardians that they might be empowered to heal them.

A wormhole is a feature of space-time that is a shortcut through four-dimensional space. The encounter with the porcupine resulted in bringing my dogs to the veterinarian where I decided to have them tested for a heartworm infection just to be sure. Only mosquitoes can transmit heartworm, but the meeting with the porcupine got us in the vet's office.

And my concern for them transformed into a body of knowledge that can serve to help all animals that suffer from heartworm disease. It has led us down an extraordinary road which has given me and my dogs a new purpose. This book supplies a shortcut for every pet owner who wants to become an advocate for their animal's health and vitality.

Two

The Thread that Connects All Life

The heartworm is only about a relationship, an ancient connection among living organisms. This relationship links many different species together into one specific purpose, the will to survive. And through the course of millennia this unifying factor has established long lasting relationships among very different organisms.

The connection between a heartworm and its host is the same as any other bond: it developed over time into what it is today. The heartworm intimately relies on other organisms to survive and has progressed into the niche it currently possesses. However, this association of the heartworm is not just between it and an animal.

If an animal that you care for has become the host of the heartworm, chances are that you have become part of that relationship. Your emotions and thoughts are now mediating amid the heartworm and your pet and seeking a resolution. You are a part of the ancient interconnection of mother nature.

And the relationship does not end with you, your pet and the heartworm, because the mosquito is also an intimate player in the game. In order for an animal to become a host to the heartworm the mosquito had to become the messenger. In fact, without the mosquito to complete its lifecycle the heartworm would disappear.

And the relationship grows, for there is living within the heartworm another parasite called Wolbachia, a hyper-parasitic microbe that relies on the worm for its survival. This bacterium takes its daily bread from the worm but includes the added benefit of possibly giving protection to the heartworm by making it more resistant to some viruses.

In a relationship, there is an exchange of energy. This relationship can also begin without any harm to the host, but when its immune system is compromised, the exchange becomes a detriment to it. The amount of harm or benefit becomes a sliding scale, relative to other influencing factors.

In nature there are many examples of symbiotic relationships that are beneficial to both. This can be a cooperative liaison amid two dissimilar living organisms such as a zebra and bacteria called intestinal and rumen protozoa. Since vertebrates (human beings to) cannot break down cellulose alone, they rely on these bacteria to do the job for them. The bacteria benefit from having an ample supply of nutrition to feed off while the zebra benefits from the added ability to absorb the fatty acids and sugars it needs to survive.

Another example of a mutualistic relationship where both are enhanced while living together in an intimate association is inside the organelles of our living cells. This is an illuminating theory that tells a story about how the components of an eukaryotic cell (cells with a nucleus) were at one time bacteria that lived in such a close union together that they eventually merged to become a member of an intracellular group of parts comprising the life of every cellular organism.

It could have been that very early in our creation, that all things were in harmony. All life cooperated in its collective goal of survival. The pathogens existed but only in a beneficial and benign way, possibly helping another with some task and taking some of its sustenance in exchange.

A FRAME OF REFERENCE

Let's stop to consider what the objective of the heartworm is. All life shares a common goal since the dawn of creation, and that is the will to survive. But when the heartworm actually kills an animal, it is actually destroying itself in the process. Something must be out of balance, since the goal of most parasites should be to live long and take advantage of remaining in a healthy host so that it can reproduce and spread beyond that animal. A heartworm survives because of its host but cannot live outside it. In light of this fact it is a logical conclusion that the heartworm does not wish to kill our pets, but to infest them quickly and then peacefully adapt to its new home.

Nevertheless, heartworms do cause disease. Many dogs, cats and ferrets die every year from a heartworm infection. No one wants their pet to have heartworm.

Nature will reveal a frame of reference to us when we have deviated too far into an unbalance with it. Contemplating the relationships of heartworm and wild animals such as wolves or coyotes can give us a clue to the best possible response in treating our pets. However, there is very little understood about how heartworms affect animals in the wild because what is noted and studied is mostly based on human or domestic animals. So far what is known about the effects of heartworm in the wild leans towards the speculative.

In general, wild animals such as wolves or coyotes exhibit a better immune response to heartworm infestations. It is hypothesized that they do not succumb to the parasite as easily as domesticated animals. Comparisons of heartworm infected coyotes have displayed a lower inflammatory response in several of their organs. However, a heartworm infected animal could meet an earlier death as a result of lowered physical stamina which would decrease its ability to forage for food.

This lower sensitivity to heartworm in wild beasts could be the reason that there have been very few if any real documented cases of the animals ever dying directly from the parasite. In almost every account, they were found dead from other natural causes. In documented studies wild animals are usually found infected with varying degrees of adult heartworms, but all perish by other means.

An African leopard in a zoo in north-eastern Italy was found to be infected with four male and two female adult heartworms during an autopsy after it died from unknown causes. Even though it was suspected that it died from a heartworm related disease there was nothing to prove that assertion. However, if heartworm was the cause of death to the leopard, it also might allude to a tendency for wild animals to die of a disease in captivity that they normally do not succumb to in their natural habitat.

Raccoon dogs are canines but look similar to raccoons. In the laboratory, they have shown mild susceptibility to infection of heartworm, yet most of the worms die and only a few grow into adulthood. Their immune system is able to keep the worms from growing more than their bodies can handle.

The ambiguity of the results of these studies allow us to reflect on the reasons why untamed vertebrates live with heartworm better than our domestic ones. For instance, there are some definite differences between dogs and wild canines even though they share a common ancestry. Domesticated canines live in an artificial world that has become their new ecosystem. These changes have been

---

"Let's stop to consider what the objective of the heartworm is. All life shares a common goal since the dawn of creation, and that is the will to survive."

---

relatively new, which has not allowed ample time for the dog to adjust to them.

Our pets usually eat food that is very different from those of its untamed forbears. And often the food does not have the nutritional or life giving quality that is required. This decreases the response of its immune system, which makes it more susceptible to an invasion of heartworm. However, the correlation between an unbalance of heartworms and nutritional status is still unclear, and any assertion made is only an assumption.

Animals in their natural habitat struggle to survive and use most of their available time and energy in finding food. They often have empty stomachs and eat questionable things, only sporadically finding nourishment. On the other hand the domestic dog or cat is usually fed regularly, but food that might be mostly corn and filled with chemical additives. It's possible that a wild animal that is only randomly fed but eats a plethora of foods might be better suited to resist an intrusion of heartworm.

ANIMAL'S RELATIONSHIP TO PLANTS

In nature, animals will gather things to digest that will help it in healing. This self medicating practice is called zoopharmacognosy, which is a relationship between the animal and its capacity to heal itself. By selecting parts of plants, berries, insects and soils animals play an active role in preventing and treating disease of every kind. They are surrounded by a living pharmacy and know exactly what prescriptions to fill.

This ability can be innate such as in finches that have displayed the ability to choose certain antibiotic compounds when given a choice and by doing so were able to cure themselves of severe disease. Or, it can be taught by parents or imitated by observation. Chimpanzees in the wild have been witnessed chewing and swallowing rough leaves of a certain plant to expel parasitic worms. It was shown that they exhibited this behavior after watching another female swallow the leaves.

Someone who has been intimately involved with a group of chimpanzees in East Africa watched in amazement as a chimp named Chausiku chew on a stick and suck out the juice then spit out the inside. He asked someone native to the area about the plant and was told that it is also sometimes ingested by the Tongwe people who use it as a very strong medicine for malaria, stomach ache and intestinal parasites. This plant was later identified by the Latin name Vernonia amygdalina, a small leafy shrub.

Also, bears in the southwest United States have a knowledge of and eat Ligusticum porteri, a plant in the carrot and parsley family which is known for its anti-parasitic properties. Bioassays of these plants have proven that they contain powerful and significant anti-microbial compounds.

Examples of zoopharmacognosy abound in every species and ecosystem, including in domestic dogs and cats and their ancestors. A study in Rhode Island that examined the stomach contents of coyotes found that wild grains, herbs, crabapples, wild grapes and other berries constituted an overall percentage of over 21 percent of their total food intake. Even though 26 percent of the coyotes were infected with heartworm, none were found that died from it.

If given the chance, domestic animals will also eat parts of wild plants to self medicate if they are suffering any physical diseases or ailments. I've seen my dogs eat many different plants when taking them into the woods to walk. They seem to know instinctively what to eat and what for. Animals that have an opportunity to spend more time in the wilderness might have a greater tendency to resist a large heartworm infection.

A PET'S RELATIONSHIP TO HEARTWORM

Our pet's relationship to heartworm has changed since it was taken out of its natural habitat millennia ago. For example, dogs today tend to get less exercise, poorer nutrition, have less available natural medicines to treat themselves, yet have a longer average life span than those in the wild. Furthermore, the process of natural selection where the strong survive to pass on their genes will not be a deciding factor for domestic dogs as it is for their ancestors.

Wild animals that survive into adulthood are usually in good physical condition after being exposed to pathogens such as heartworm that can unfortunately kill some domestic ones. In comparison, even though domestic dogs can live long lives, their vitality overall might be compromised by over-breeding and excessive vaccinations.

Considering the deteriorated relationship that our pets now have with heartworm, we can proceed with foresight into an action plan to assure that their health will be compromised as little as possible. By using their wild ancestor's health as a model to shape our treatment plan and fully acknowledging our domestic creature's higher susceptibility to heartworm, we can better help our pet's natural response to repelling the parasite.

We need treatments that will successfully negate the antagonistic effects of heartworm without further endangering the animal's current state of health. If we administer them medicines that gradually lower its immune system, we are only opening doors to further problems down the line.

Heartworm is a parasitic worm that sometimes mutates into strains that can effectively sidestep the current treatments created by big pharmaceutical companies. However, the benefits and negatives of modern medicines and natural ones need to be weighed by one factor: the overall health and quality of life our pets must have.

The relationships among ourselves, our pets and other organisms are fluid and constantly changing. And by developing better and less abrasive medicines while not ignoring nature's pharmacy and our pet's innate ability to defend itself from disease, we can move forward into a better future for ourselves and our animals.

HEARTWORM'S MANY ACQUAINTANCES

The heartworm, also known as Dirofilaria immitis, is a parasitic roundworm that moves from host to host by the means of a mosquito. For a "host" the heartworm can live and reproduce in more creatures than just wild or domestic animals, it can also inhabit a human being. However, humans are considered to be aberrant hosts (heartworm will rarely develop into adults). Also, heartworm usually don't cause significant harm to aberrant hosts since the worms die off very quickly.

Midway aberrant hosts and definitive hosts (canines) are animals that are imperfect hosts to heartworm. These include animals such as cats and ferrets where heartworms are able to develop into adults but in much smaller amounts, usually never exceeding five adults. In contrast, larger canines are capable of harboring hundreds of adult worms if bitten enough times by infected mosquitoes.

Over time, more animals are identified that can be infected by adult heartworms. This is in part to increased testing and an increased range of the heartworm. As the temperature of the planet rises, mosquitoes will be able to transmit heartworms to places once out of reach.

EXAMPLES OF DEFINITIVE HOSTS:

- The coyote (Canis latrans)
- The grey wolf (Canis lupus)
- The domestic dog (Canis lupus familiaris)

EXAMPLES OF IMPERFECT HOSTS:

- The harbor seal (Phoca vitulina)
- The snow leopard (Uncia uncia)
- The Humboldt Penguin (Spheniscus humboldti)
- The ferret (Mustela putorius furo)
- The lion (Panthera leo)
- The jaguar (Panthera onca)
- The domestic cat (Felis silvestris catus)

EXAMPLES OF ABERRANT HOSTS:

- The raccoon (Procyon lotor)
- The North American black bear (Ursus americanus)
- The North American porcupine (Erethizon dorsatum)
- The Human (Homo sapien)

THREE

LADIES AND GENTLEMEN

THE HEARTWORM IS A PARASITIC ROUNDWORM THAT infects its host by the bite of the mosquito. It lives within the host but cannot survive outside it. Again, the heartworm's official name is Dirofilaria immitis, and is part of a family of nematodes that are found in diverse parts of the world and in many species of animals. These nematodes are an increasing problem in the world of human beings, especially in poorer countries.

Nematodes have their origin rooted in ancient history. They were among the first to emerge after bacteria, protozoa and fungi and as time advanced they became a parasite to marine invertebrates (animals that live in water and without a vertebrae).

They are usually very small, but have functional bodies with developed muscles and digestive systems. They even exhibit the capability of learned behavior making them a little smarter than previously imagined.

They are everywhere, and may even comprise 90 percent of organisms on the ocean floor. They have adapted to every ecosystem on earth, from the highest to the lowest elevations, in marine and fresh water, in polar regions and tropics and in all extreme of temperatures.

Nathan Cobb, who is described as the father of nematology, has said, "In short, if all the matter in the universe except the nematodes were swept away, our world would still be dimly recognizable, and if, as disembodied spirits, we could then investigate it, we should find its mountains, hills, vales, rivers, lakes, and oceans represented by a film of nematodes. The location of towns would be decipherable, since for every massing of human beings there would be a corresponding massing of certain nematodes. Trees would still stand in ghostly rows representing our streets and highways. The location of the various plants and animals would still be decipherable, and, had we sufficient knowledge, in many cases even their species could be determined by an examination of their erstwhile nematode parasites."

By studying ancient fossils of nematodes that have been perfectly preserved in Baltic amber, a clearer picture of their development and adaptations over time emerges. Actually, they have fundamentally changed very little since time began. They have just become habituated to survive by emerging as parasites of an incredibly diverse number of animals and organisms including plants. It is estimated that there are over one million different species of nematodes living in the world today.

There are many free-living nematodes as well, which play a very important role of breaking down waste into usable soil. By feeding on fungi, algae, animals, dead organisms, fecal matter and living tissues they transform the earth's dregs and renew its resources. Nematodes can also be used in important future advancements in organic and sustainable agriculture.

LOOKS AREN'T EVERYTHING

D. immitis (heartworm) has a creamy white, cylindrical, and slender body, and its skin has a shiny and reflective quality. The translucent appearing skin acts as a protective coating against the host's immune proteins and cells. Bands of muscles run along its body from top to bottom, making the worm look rigid and firm.

Heartworm include both sexes, the male and female. However, the adult male is smaller measuring around 12-16 cm in comparison to the female, which measures around 25-30 cm. The tail of the male coils at the end, not unlike a corkscrew, and is endowed with testis while the female possesses ovaries.

The heartworm's offspring, which are called microfilariae, resemble their parents but are microscopic in size, usually about six microns. For comparison, they are similar in width to red blood cells. Microfilariae can be found in the blood all over the body in an infected host. Also, they can live in other fluids such as urine, cerebrospinal fluid and fluids in the abdominal areas and lungs.

Unlike adults, microfilariae have tapered heads, straight tails and lack fully developed organs. Microfilariae wiggle in place but lack any forward motion. Surprisingly, they can sometimes live past 24 months in age.

Adult D. immitis can sense its external world using sense organs. Setae organs detect motion while amphid organs can detect chemicals such as pheromones which are used to attract males.

Just as every other organism, Dirofilaria immitis (heartworm) must eat to survive. The developing larvae dine directly on the cells of the malpighian tubes of the mosquito. In its other stages of development, the heartworm feeds on the blood of its host.

In a dog heartworm can live past six years in age. But their life span is shortened in smaller animals like a cat or ferret.

TO BE OR NOT TO BE

Dirofilaria immitis is sometimes considered a parasitoid because it can sometimes kill its host. A parasitoid is an organism that is similar to a parasite. It spends most of its life living within a single host living off of and using the host's resources to survive. However, the difference lies in how it treats its host. The parasitoid ultimately sterilizes or kills its host and sometimes even consumes it.

Dirofilaria immitis (heartworm) does not consume its host, but sometimes it can contribute to the destruction of it. However, the true definition of parasitoid includes the fact that after it kills its host, it becomes a free-living organism. Since this obviously does not apply to heartworm, using the term "parasitoid" is an unfair comparison.

Also, the fact that heartworm can be the straw that sometimes breaks the camels back does not mean that they are made to do so. Even though heartworm usually contribute bad effects to an animal's health does not confirm that this is a part of its function.

From the heartworm's point of view it is completely illogical to cause the death of its host. Not only does the heartworm gain nothing from this, but it also loses its own chance of continued survival.

A COOPERATIVE MOSQUITO

The mosquito is paramount in the lifecycle of Dirofilaria immitis. Not only does the heartworm depend on it to spread it from host to host, it also completes a phase of its own development within the body of the mosquito.

This level of dependence and cooperation that Dirofilaria immitis relies on to survive is astonishing. It's clear that the heartworm gains immensely from the mosquito, yet its probable that the mosquito gains nothing from carrying the heartworm larvae.

Mosquitoes of several species such as the Aedes, Anopholes and Culex are able to remain unaffected by viruses because their immune system corrupts the viruses genetic coding. Mosquitoes are also unaffected by most parasites, yet it is unknown how this happens. It is probable that their immune system also plays a role in keeping parasites from harming their bodies. The bacteria Wolbachia might also play a role in keeping some mosquitoes free of harm by the heartworm larvae and other pathogens.

"Microfilarial periodicity" means that microfilariae in a host's blood becomes greater in number at certain times of the day. This is a clever way of boosting the amount of microfilariae that the mosquito ingests by targeting the time of day that the mosquito feeds the most, usually in the evening.

In addition to heartworm, mosquitoes can also be host to other parasites and viruses as well. Malaria, spread by the mosquito, is at the top of the list as a cause of death to human beings, infecting millions and killing thousands every year.

Interestingly, it has recently been discovered that a parasitic bacteria called Wolbachia, which infects both heartworm and mosquitoes, can reduce the spread of malaria. Scientists have discovered mosquitoes infected with Wolbachia cannot carry infectious bacteria such as malaria at the same time. But it seems that infecting certain species of mosquitoes with Wolbachia that transmit these diseases to human beings, is a hard task to accomplish.

Alternatively, some scientists are working on altering the genetic structure of human disease carrying mosquitoes making them benign to humans. What is not discussed is the cost of genetically manufacturing nature, are humans really prepared to play God?

A PERSISTENT GUEST - WOLBACHIA

Wolbachia pipientis is an intercellular bacteria that live inside the cells of some nematode worms of the Onchocercidae family, which include Dirofilaria immitis and a high percentage of arthropods. How many species it inhabits is unknown, since Wolbachia has been mostly studied relative to disease. Since Wolbachia is often beneficial to its host, these mutualistic relationships are only beginning to be studied. Currently, it is estimated that more than five million species are infected with the Wolbachia bacteria.

It is fascinating that both the heartworm and the mosquito harbor the same bacteria. It could have been that in ancient days, and while the heartworm was progressing in its life stages inside the mosquito, that Wolbachia somehow moved in.

Wolbachia belongs to a class of Rickettsiales bacteria in the Anaplasmataceae family. Most of those bacteria are parasites and causes of disease in plants, animals and human beings. Though there are some exceptions, Wolbachia have been found to be mostly beneficial in nature to their hosts.

The Wolbachia that live inside the heartworm are endosymbionts, which means that neither they nor their host survive without each other. If one or the other was to die, that would cause the death of both. If the Wolbachia that lives within the heartworm were to die, the worm would die with them. But first it would make the heartworm weaker and unable to produce offspring. This is why researchers are currently testing ways of eliminating Wolbachia as a much safer and efficient way of treating heartworm disease. This is the future of heartworm treatment, and precisely why more and more doctors recommend eliminating Wolbachia first, which is covered later in this book.

Surely the relationship between these bacteria and their hosts is an ancient one. It's probable that the ancestors of all Rickettsiales bacteria were an intracellular pathogens, and their descendent Wolbachia was tamed into a beneficial symbiotic relationship with its hosts. In fact, Wolbachia has established some very clever ways to ensure its own survival through the ages.

In arthropods and the mosquito, in which Wolbachia was first discovered, there exists some fascinating reproductive manipulations caused by the bacteria. Since Wolbachia can only pass their offspring to female arthropods, they have devised a way to manipulate whether an egg hatches into a male or female. By directly killing males or turning males into females the Wolbachia ensures that it will be maternally inherited by the bug's female descendants.

Alternatively, by the process of cytoplasmic incompatibility, Wolbachia can cause infected males to become unable to reproduce with uninfected females or females infected with a different strain of Wolbachia. An even more intriguing way Wolbachia manipulates the sexes of some arthropods is by using parthenogenesis, wherein females can produce asexually; meaning without males. In fact, scientists have suggested that parthenogenesis is always attributable to Wolbachia.

Some species of the scorpion, also an arthropod, have been found to carry Wolbachia. And because some scorpions can produce through parthenogenesis, I propose that they can do so, only because of the Wolbachia that live within their cells.

Another way that Wolbachia might ensure its continued survival is by contributing to the health of their host. It has been discovered that Wolbachia keeps its host healthy by inducing a greater resistance to other natural pathogens. This can be seen in some mosquitoes that have a enhanced resistance to disease causing agents such as dengue and malaria. This has also been shown to be true for the fly called Drosophila melanogaster, in which the bacteria Wolbachia induces a resistance to natural and viral pathogens. As I stated earlier, scientists are learning to take advantage of this phenomenon by engineering Wolbachia to infect mosquitoes that carry human disease, thereby making the mosquitoes immune and unable to spread the infection.

Wolbachia are similar to viruses, in that they share genetic material with their hosts by a function called horizontal gene transfer. The transfer of genes at the cellular level is ancient and has a huge significance to the procession of life since time began. This has caused some peculiar exchanges of needed metabolites between Wolbachia and some of their hosts.

For example, scientists have found that the genome of Wolbachia to be very small and that they derive most of the building blocks

---

"This is why researchers are currently testing ways of eliminating Wolbachia as a much safer and efficient way of treating heartworm disease."

---

for life from their hosts. This is common with horizontal gene transfer, but what is unique is that in exchange for these amino acids, Wolbachia sometimes provides some essential metabolites that the host must have to function.

A good example of this intercellular commerce is between Dirofilaria immitis and Wolbachia. There is evidence that Wolbachia provides essential metabolite molecules for the fertility, survival and development of Dirofilaria immitis. When the Wolbachia are eliminated, embryogenesis is halted and the worm is unable to produce microfilariae. Also, it will slowly die without the necessary chemicals it needs to sustain its life.

Wolbachia might also help protect the heartworm from being discovered by the animal's immune system which would try to kill and expel it. It seems that Wolbachia stay dormant in the heartworm's early life stages, then multiply rapidly after becoming a young adult and exposed to the macrophage cells of the animal's immune system.

The discovery of Wolbachia in Dirofilaria immitis is of great significance. It will provide us with new and better ways of testing for heartworm infection. And, by tracking when Wolbachia is eliminated from the worm, we will be able to test and find the best time to deliver treatments. In addition, treating heartworm by treating Wolbachia leads to much safer and efficient remedies to heartworm disease. This exciting information is later expounded on in the next chapter.

STAGES OF A HEARTWORM'S LIFECYCLE

Dirofilaria immitis goes through five stages of larval development within its lifespan, starting with stage L1 and ending in L5. The heartworm uses the mosquito similar to a womb where it can develop and mature, and is wholly dependent on it to begin its life cycle.

Depending on the host, the stages can progress slightly slower or faster than it does in the dog. For example, in the cat the heartworm develops a month or two later than in the dog.

The adult worms in infected animals produce offspring called microfilariae that circulate in the animal's blood. These microfilariae are in the first stage of their lifecycle called L1. Within two weeks or longer, the microfilariae can develop into stage L2, depending in the temperature.

Development within the mosquito is dependent on the temperature which must remain at or above 27°C (80°F) for at least two weeks. When the temperature reaches 14°C (57°F) or below, their life cycle is completely halted. This is important as it reveals when heartworm preventative is doubly important.

When the larvae have reached the mouth area of the mosquito they have progressed to the infective stage L3 in their development. At this point they are ready to be deposited onto the surface of an animal so that they can find their way into the subcutaneous tissue below the skin. They actively burrow through the wound the mosquito made and go under the skin to progress onward into its next stage of development.

Once established in the subcutaneous tissue, the larvae develop into their fourth stage called L4. This stage lasts from one day and up to two weeks or longer. Then for the next three or four months the larvae transform into immature adult heartworms as they move through the muscle of the animal's body.

By the time they have penetrated into the pulmonary arterioles and the right side of the heart, they are already immature adults in the last stage of their development called L5. In the dog this can be anywhere from one to 250 worms while in the cat and ferret there will only be a few at most.

The mosquito can only infect an animal with a couple heartworm larvae at a time. If that animal is never bitten again by an infectious mosquito their heartworm infection will not increase. Heartworm cannot reproduce inside of the host, but need the mosquito to increase their number.

While in the pulmonary arteries and the right ventricle of the heart, the heartworms mature into sexually mature adults. The female produces a pheromone that is used to attract the male to copulate. The male will then wrap its coiled tail around the female's genital pore to reproduce.

Here the developmental stages of the heartworm start from the beginning. The microfilariae born from the female heartworm will circulate in the animal's blood and will later progress into their later stages after a mosquito ingests them. Then, if the mosquito bites another host after the microfilariae have developed into stage L3, the process can start all over again.

It's possible that puppies can be born with microfilariae passed to them from their mother in the womb. But it's comforting to know that they pose no threat to the newborn. A mosquito needs to be the intermediary between one host and the other and without that bridge the heartworm larvae cannot develop. Blood transfusions will not pose any risk either, since there is no mosquito involved.

FOUR

THE RAIN OF RUIN

THE IMPACT OF HEARTWORM DISEASE CAN BE insidious. It can rack havoc on an animal's body, starting an avalanche of clinical symptoms. Even a small heartworm infection in a dog can produce symptoms. But the response of a host's body to heartworm disease varies greatly, depending on health, size, age and breed.

Although heartworm disease can be deadly, not all animals will yield to the parasite. Some will spontaneously recover their health while rejecting the parasite from their body. Also, prevention and treatment are readily available and effective.

Since D. immitis is most comfortable in a canine, we will use that model as a starting point for the characteristic disease progression it causes. Once we see clearly how the disease affects a dog, we can compare those to effects in other animals.

THE HEARTWORM'S JOURNEY

As soon as they enter a dog's body, immature heartworms instinctively travel through the tissue towards the caudal lung lobes, where the caudal pulmonary arteries are located. The term "caudal" means posterior and in this case translates to mean near the surface of the lungs. Although heartworm seem to favor the right lung, it's possible that their distribution may also be unilateral (both sides). The heartworm's inclination to journey to the pulmonary arteries is very powerful, and will even re-migrate there if transplanted into another animal.

"Even a small heartworm infection in a dog can produce symptoms."

Once the larvae grow large enough, they will drill through the tissues of blood vessels and go inside. The moment they enter the interior of the artery they start causing damage. This marks the beginning of the cascading effects of disease inside the host's body. Similar to the first domino knocking over the next, the damage caused in the pulmonary arteries starts a chain reaction that can ravage the rest of the body.

As the infection persists or the number of heartworms increase, the farther they move down the pulmonary arteries toward the right ventricle and atrium of the heart. D. immitis tends to hang around the bifurcation (fork in the road) of the large pulmonary arteries. Later, when these worms die, they will be pushed back to the furthest edges of the lung in the same place they first entered.

Injury to the Pulmonary Arteries

The initial injury is initiated by the presence of the worms inside the lumen (inside tube) of the arteries. The surface of these pulmonary arteries suffer trauma which cause lesions to appear in only a few days. The constant presence of the foreign body of the heartworm scratches and disturbs the surface of the artery. This injury is even more damaging when the heartworm dies, especially when they die all at once during treatment.

The arteries normal white and reflective surface is interchanged by a purple, wrinkled and scarred one. They become dilated (expand) and the walls of the mucosa (inside of artery) thicken. These lesions grow inward until they can just barley accommodate the heartworm. The smaller diameter of the arteries blocks blood flow and increases the work load of the heart.

The process that causes this thickening of the arterial walls is similar to how the skin reacts to a wound like a scrape or a burn. The lesions will initiate a healing process where platelets in the blood will cover the wound and form something similar to a scab. What is really happening is an inflammatory response that is initiated by the host's body to heal itself.

When a heartworm dies a different kind of lesion is produced called a granulomatous lesion which can be much more devastating. Both type of lesions are similar to those produced by arteriosclerosis (hardening of the arteries) in human beings, but do not develop accumulations of fatty acids, cholesterol or calcium.

The cells on the normal surfaces of the pulmonary arteries are well organized, and oriented in the same direction of blood flow. They form a tight fitting barrier that does not allow fluid such as blood to leak out. Once D. immitis enters the artery it immediately begins to cause the endothelial cells (thin layer of cells that line the arterial walls) to disorganize, become swollen and spread apart. The body then activates its immune system and sends in leukocyte cells (white blood cells that defend the body from disease) that adhere to the walls of the artery.

The tissue underneath the wall of the artery becomes exposed and platelets in the blood adhere to the surface. This initiates rapid cell division causing the inward migration of smooth muscle cells. The surface layer of the arterial wall is lost and the smooth muscle cells become orientated towards the surface.

The arterial walls transform from smooth to mountainous. The barrier that was designed to keep fluid from leaking into the surrounding tissue has been undermined, and edema (accumulation of fluid) in the lungs further worsens the condition.

The changes of the arterial surface and the narrowing of the inside diameter begin at the location of the heartworm, while the artery expands to accommodate it. This is most severe in the distant caudal arteries, which become pruned and tortuous. This is in contrast to a normal dog's arteries which gradually taper, have a smooth interior and exterior, and are linear (straight) in shape.

The narrowing of the arteries lessens the amount of blood flow that can reach the lungs. As the pulmonary arteries get obstructed, the flow of blood becomes sluggish. This causes the bronchial arteries to make up the difference in blood flow.

Since the job of the pulmonary arteries is to carry deoxygenated blood to the lungs to become oxygenated, their decreased ability to do so produces a lack of oxygen in the host's body. Lack of oxygen in the body is called hypoxia, and can cause bluing on the surfaces of the skin.

Also, the failure of the left ventricle of the heart to sufficiently remove blood from the pulmonary circulation gives rise to pulmonary edema. This is where fluid in the air spaces of the lungs accumulates and impairs oxygen and carbon dioxide exchange which produces a multitude of respiratory problems such as coughing.

Since some of the caudal pulmonary arteries become blocked or narrow, they become non-functional. Some arteries are not used until they are needed, like when the dog exercises or becomes active. A dog with pulmonary blockages might not appear tired until it needs those extra vessels to oxygenate the blood. As a result the dog will tire quickly after it becomes active. In advanced stages of heartworm disease the dog might be short of breath even at rest.

Another factor that could contribute to the narrowing of the pulmonary arteries are circulating filarial factors such as antigens which are produced by D. immitis. These chemical compositions actually add to some of the constriction of the muscles inside the arteries. It has been shown in the laboratory that aspirin can markedly reduce this constriction.

Later in the disease sequence, the problems in the pulmonary arteries induced by the live heartworm escalate into pulmonary hypertension. This is a condition where the heart has to pump against an unnatural resistance to the blood flow going to the lungs. This continual counteraction the heart experiences causes its walls to stretch, thicken and harden to compensate for the greater pressures inside. Also, the heart now has to pump much faster to make up for its reduced output. As the heart's work load intensifies, the likelihood that it will eventually fail increases. Pulmonary hypertension leads to the next step in the disease progression, congestive heart failure.

THE HEART'S LAST STAND

During late stages of a heartworm infection, congestive heart failure can occur when the right ventricle of the heart becomes overloaded and cannot supply enough oxygenated blood to the body. This happens as a result of the extra resistance to blood flow that the heart encounters from the narrowing of the pulmonary arteries.

As blood accumulates in the venous system and becomes backed up, the heart cannot pump enough blood forward to bring deoxygenated blood back to the lungs. This can cause a multitude of problems and symptoms, the worst of which is death.

The increased arterial pressure will cause the muscle of the heart and pulmonary arteries to stretch and then to thicken. This bulge can be seen in a radiograph (x-ray image) and is indicative of heartworm disease late in its progression. These changes can also cause the heart's natural rhythm to become delayed and abnormal.

The accumulation of fluid in air spaces of the lung can make the dog's stomach look bulgy and swollen. Also, the liver can enlarge which is a sign of congestive heart failure when it is seen on a radiograph.

The increased volume overload exacerbates the dog's intolerance to exercise. Although the problems of blood flow and blockages in the pulmonary arteries are serious, congestive heart failure trumps all other damage the disease can cause.

An animal that is suffering from the effects of cardiopulmonary disease will show a number of symptoms. Coughing is most common and is initiated by the irritation of the respiratory passageway. Shortness of breath causes rapid breathing. The heart will pump faster at rest and the animal will tire quickly when exercising. Fainting and coughing blood are more serious signs of a more progressed disease.

Both pulmonary hypertension and congestive heart failure can be diagnosed by taking x-rays of the chest and examining the anatomy for signs of change. A tell tale sign of pulmonary hypertension in dogs is an enlargement of the right side of the heart, and an expansion of the main pulmonary artery.

An x-ray can show obstructions of blood flow in the more distant pulmonary arteries as well. They look like broken branches coming off of a larger artery. These are areas not receiving enough blood to keep the tissue alive. Also, the lungs can look cloudy on the x-ray due to the increased density of the smaller arteries.

The probability of heartworm disease is high if 2 or 3 of those indications on the radiograph are present. Sometimes a veterinarian will use an electrocardiograph (EKG) to detect right ventricular hypertrophy (hardening and stretching of heart muscles) if the disease has progressed far enough. It may also show abnormal electrical activity or an irregular heartbeat.

Traditional treatment of heartworm disease is constantly evolving. As new and better ways are discovered, the drug companies and governments dance around patents and profits. But because of this, the best treatment for that animal might be discarded for something more lucrative.

For many years an arsenic based compound called an adulticide was given to the dog to kill all the heartworms at once. This is still the main protocol in most veterinarian offices. But, the company that makes the only drug approved in America by the FDA called Melarsomine, ran out of stock. Since then an anti-parasitic called ivermectin and an antibiotic called doxycycline are the drugs of choice.

If there are disease symptoms those are usually treated first along with exercise restrictions before the treatment begins. Corticosteroid drugs such as prednisolone are sometimes prescribed to counter inflammation. But prednisolone inhibits clearance of heartworm fragments which lessens resolution and healing of the arterial disease. Aspirin seems to be the better choice to reduce inflammation that causes the narrowing of the arteries.

Congestive heart failure gets some additional treatment. Pulmonary vasodilators such as hydralazine, that relax the arteries allowing more blood flow and lowering blood pressure are sometimes used. But they are considered potentially dangerous and are given only when extensive monitoring can be done. Diuretics are also used to remove excess fluid from the body.

TWO'S COMPANY, THREE'S A CROWD

In areas of the world where heartworm is very endemic (common), animals can be infected with heartworm larvae many times from mosquitoes repeatedly biting them. This causes a symptom called vena caval syndrome, where many heartworm congest the right atrium and vena cava of the heart. A mass of D. immitis literally fills the right side of the heart, and can extend into the liver through the vena cava.

The clogging of the heart with worms produces similar symptoms seen in congestive heart failure. But with the advancement of the disease to this point, it is probable that pulmonary hypertension and congestive heart failure are developing and producing effects of their own as well.

In addition, vena caval syndrome can produce liver and kidney malfunction, the refusal to eat, right-sided cardiac murmur, respiratory distress, weakness and seriously affect the functionality of the heart valves. As blood flows through the mass of worms some of the red blood cells are damaged or destroyed which causes anemia. This will result in turning the urine a shade of red.

Vena caval syndrome can also cause disseminated intravascular coagulation (DIC) which is when the blood begins to coagulate in the small blood vessels all over the body. This coagulation causes many proteins and blood platelets to be used up. Since their numbers are low this brings about uncontrolled bleeding from wounds, in the intestines and respiratory tract. Organs may also malfunction as a result of disrupted blood flow.

Although DIC is dire in most other diseases, there is a much better rate of survival when caused by heartworm disease. DIC can also be initiated by treatment of heartworm disease using an adulticide compound. This kills all the worms at once which results in massive damage to the pulmonary tissues and arteries.

Although vena caval syndrome is a serious problem to an animal's health, it can be successfully treated. In advanced stages the worms can be removed surgically, pulling them out through the jugular vein. And mild symptoms can be treated with supportive aids while working on eliminating the worms from their body.

STRANGE AND FARAWAY PLACES

Sometimes, a heartworm will get disorientated and travel far away from where it intended to go. This could happen because the heartworm is not familiar with the territory, such as when it infects an aberrant host (diverging from the normal type) such as a horse, bear or human being. This can produce all kinds of irregular symptoms as the tissue attempts to eliminate the worm.

D. immits can also end up in faraway places of a dog's anatomy as well. Even though the heartworm knows this territory intimately, sometimes for unknown reasons it can get lost. It could be that the animal has an unique chemistry or physical structure that deviates the heartworm from its path to the pulmonary arteries and right side of the heart.

In the dog, heartworms have been found in the eyes, central nervous system, the systemic arteries and the skin. Many problems can occur when heartworms find themselves in these places, especially in the central nervous system (including the brain) and arteries.

AN EYE FOR AN EYE

There have been a few documented cases of dogs with immature adult heartworms swimming in the fluid-filled space inside the eye between the iris and the cornea's innermost surface. Often, the anterior chamber of the eye becomes cloudy and bloodshot.

It seems that heartworms fiercely oppose light from any source. When light is shined on them while they are exposed in the eye's chamber they violently thrash about. They also recoil from the blunt metal instrument that the surgeon uses to extract them from the eye.

The dogs that have been diagnosed with ocular heartworm infections often do not have any other adult heartworms or circulating microfilariae found in their bodies. These dogs might have unique characteristics that cause the heartworms to find other places to inhabit.

Dogs that need the removal of a heartworm from their eye often recover without any permanent impairment. Unlike river blindness caused by the nematode Onchocerciasis in human beings, time will usually reverse any damage caused to the ocular tissue by the worm.

HEARTWORM AND THE CENTRAL NERVOUS SYSTEM

Heartworms have been found in the cerebral arteries and the ventricles of the brains of dogs. Though rare, the symptoms can be bizarre.

As the adults grow in size they can cause intermittent convulsions, lack of coordination, blindness, erratic behavior, constricted pupils, irritability, vomiting, lethargy, abnormal salivation, hyperactivity, an inability to stand and death. Dogs have improved when given antibiotics, mannitol or corticosteroids. Surgical removal of the heartworms from the brain should allow reversal of signs but carries risk.

Some dogs have been seen with a paralysis of one or more of their hind legs. This can be induced in dogs with heartworms within their spinal canal around the intervertebral disks.

Detecting and diagnosing the reason for the paralysis can be difficult. Radiographs and electroencephalograms will not be effective so cerebrospinal fluid analysis and ultrasounds are used to pinpoint the cause. A procedure called hemilaminectomy is sometimes used in a veterinarian hospital as treatment by alleviating pressure on the nerves in the spinal canal.

HEARTWORMS IN THE SYSTEMIC ARTERIES

Heartworms can also show up in the systemic arteries, especially in the hind legs of a dog. This can cause one or both of the rear legs to be unusable, similar to the effect of a heartworm in the spinal canal. Limbs can be painful when touched and feel cold due to a lack of blood flow. Arteriograms are used for diagnostics and surgical removal of the heartworm is performed in a veterinarian hospital.

UNDER THE SKIN

Sometimes a painful abscess can form because of a live immature adult heartworm living under the skin. It can be surgically removed by lancing the abscess and removing the heartworm.

THE OCCULT HEARTWORM DISEASE

Some dogs that are hypersensitive to heartworms and have more antibodies than average can have an occult heartworm disease infection. This means that when female worms living in the pulmonary arteries and capillaries give birth to microfilariae, the body will identify them as invaders and signal them to be destroyed by the bodies immune system. The harmful effects of the microfilariae dying in the vessels of the lungs causes the quickening of pulmonary hypertension.

The dead microfilariae become stuck in the small blood vessels of the lung which provokes granulomatous lesions to form. These granulomatous lesions are nodules in the pulmonary arteries that exacerbate the narrowing of the vessels resulting in greater resistance to blood flow and causing an increase of pulmonary hypertension.

Although occult heartworm disease accounts for roughly a quarter of infections in canines, they produce a particular insidious form of heartworm disease. Damaging occult infections are much more common in a cat's anatomy, due to their well tuned immune system.

Occult heartworm disease should not be confused with an occult heartworm infection. This can disorientate many people since there seems to be very little clear information online and in print on the subject. Many sources clump the two terms together without any distinction.

To be clear, an occult heartworm infection occurs when there are no microfilariae born to females due to an all male or female population, females that become sterile, and older heartworms. Occult heartworm *disease* occurs when microfilariae are actually born but are immediately destroyed by the animal's immune system. The granulomatous lesions formed in this process hasten the onset of pulmonary hypertension.

COLLATERAL DAMAGE

As heartworm disease progresses, more of the organs and tissues are negatively influenced by the changes in the pulmonary system of the dog. This initial pulmonary disease causes a landslide of changes in the blood chemistry, the liver, and the kidneys.

BLOOD CHANGES

Dogs with advanced heartworm disease are usually anemic. When the blood flows through the arteries the red blood cells can be traumatized or destroyed as they pass over the foreign body of the worm. Anemia can cause weakness and fatigue and in extreme cases, produce heart problems as it tries to compensate for the lack of oxygen in the blood.

White blood cells defend the body from both infectious disease and foreign material and will increase when confronted with the heartworm. Both eosinophilia and basoshilia cells increase during heartworm disease.

Sodium also increases in the blood. Because the body is out of balance, it makes sense that everything else will be to. That is why dogs with heartworm disease should eat a restricted diet with very little salt.

When the body attempts to repair the lesions on the endothelial surfaces in the pulmonary arteries caused by the heartworm, it recruits platelets in the blood to cover the wounds. Platelets are small cell fragments that live up to 9 days and circulate in the blood of all mammals. As they get used up repairing and covering the damage done by the heartworms, the platelets cannot be recruited to be used in other places they are needed. Bleeding can occur in areas that otherwise would not.

The major catalyst that produces pulmonary hypertension is the platelet adhesion to the endothelial surfaces inside the pulmonary arteries. While the platelets adhere to the surface, they create a kind of scab that narrows the passageway of the arteries and creates resistance to blood flow backing up the blood and increasing the pressure. If this process could be interrupted, then the major disease causing symptoms would cease.

The mechanism that causes the platelet adhesion which produces heartworm disease can be turned off. It was discovered in the 1980's that a low dose of aspirin will actually stop the platelet adhesion and allow healing to occur in the blood vessels even while the adult heartworms are still present.

HEARTWORM AND THE LIVER

The presence of heartworms can also negatively influence the liver of a canine. It seems that 10% of heartworm infections have elevated liver enzymes and cholesterol produced by too much strain on the liver.

The liver can enlarge because of the pressure put on it from pulmonary hypertension. Also, heartworms can pack into the caudal vena cava and extend into the veins inside the liver. It's important to feed an animal a nutritious diet to support their liver function.

HEARTWORM AND THE KIDNEYS

Problems with the functioning of the kidneys affects a lower percentage of dogs with heartworm disease than problems with the liver does. Kidney malfunction usually produces proteinuria which is an excess protein in the urine causing it to become foamy.

A renal condition called azotemia also affects dogs with heartworm disease but is less common. It gives rise to higher percentages of nitrogen compounds such as urea, creatinine and waste materials. However, these waste materials can also cause multiple symptoms such as fatigue, decreased alertness, confusion, pale skin, a rapid pulse, dry mouth and thirst.

The kidneys will also have to cope with increased filtering tasks. The imbalance of compounds in the blood and the addition of by-products of the immune system can elicit lesions in the filtering anatomy of the kidneys.

It's important to give dogs a lot of water, especially when they are having renal problems. Giving them water soluble vitamins such as vitamin B and vitamin C is a good idea and will help keep their electrolytes balanced.

HEARTWORM DISEASE IN CATS

Heartworm disease in cats has been on the rise, possibly due to an increased awareness of the disease. Although D. immitis prefers a canine as its ideal host, the cat can also serve as a place for it to live, even if the conditions are less than optimal. Similar to the dog, heartworms will congregate in the distant pulmonary arteries in the lungs. Because the feline is a foreign environment for D. immits, the worm can sometimes end up in faraway places such as in the central nervous system.

However, a cat's body will seldom permit heartworms to live into adulthood, as its immune system will usually recognize the intruders and destroy them before they can get a foothold. This is a hostile environment to a heartworm, yet sometimes they can survive and cause problems for the cat.

The smooth protective coating used to sidestep the immunity of the host that D. immits has on the surface of its body, cannot easily fool the cat's defense system that is ultra sensitive to these types of invaders. Although this protects felines from some infections, it ultimately gives rise to the primary disease mechanism of heartworm in the cat.

Although live heartworms will cause lesions in the pulmonary arteries, the fundamental mechanism of heartworm disease happens when the immunity of the cat ultimately kills the heartworm. As the heartworm's body disintegrates in the pulmonary arteries, it induces a pulmonary thromboembolism which quickens the thickening of the inside of the pulmonary arteries. In a feline, D. immitis has a life span of only half of that in a canine and the pulmonary hypertension and arterial blockages that result from the heartworm's early death can be devastating.

In addition, occult heartworm disease can be produced if female worms give birth to microfilariae. The immune system will identify and kill most of the offspring almost immediately after they are born. This will cause granulomatous lesions in the distant pulmonary arteries to form which will hasten the onset of pulmonary hypertension and can eventually lead to congestive heart failure.

Although these symptoms can ultimately cause the death of a cat, sometimes it can happen suddenly and without any warning or foreknowledge of the disease.

Heartworms do not grow as large as they do in a dog due to the cat's smaller arteries. Also, only a few worms can infect a cat at a time.

Pulmonary hypertension in a cat will produce similar symptoms as in a dog. As the pressure rises and the arterial flow becomes blocked the heart has to work harder to oxygenate the body. This will also produce problems in the blood, and kidney and liver functioning.

"Although live heartworms will cause lesions in the pulmonary arteries, the fundamental mechanism of heartworm disease in a cat happens when the immunity of the cat ultimately kills the heartworm."

A new term has recently emerged called "heartworm associated respiratory disease" or HARD abbreviated. This is common in cats because they are more susceptible to occult heartworm disease which produces symptoms similar to asthma or allergic bronchitis.

Although exercise intolerance is uncommon, coughing, vomiting, weight loss, refusal to eat, tiredness and harsh breathing sounds could be signs of the disease. Neurological problems such as tremors or unbalanced coordination could result from a heartworm infection in the nervous system.

Pulmonary hypertension is detected as enlarged lobar pulmonary arteries on a x-ray radiograph. Although the main pulmonary artery enlarges just as in a dog, it is difficult to see in a radiograph because of its location in a cat's anatomy. An x-ray radiograph can also help diagnose heartworm disease in a cat by revealing cloudy areas in the lung tissue.

Treatment of heartworm disease in cats has gravitated more to supportive aids to improve the animal's overall health. Exercise restrictions, diuretics and corticosteroids are used in more extreme cases.

Because it is so dangerous when the worms die in a feline, treatment involving adulticide that kills the worms directly has been fatal to cats. But it has been demonstrated that ivermectin will kill the adult worms gradually.

Sometimes the worms need to be removed surgically. This is can happen when the heartworms arrive in distant corners of a cat's anatomy.

HEARTWORM DISEASE IN THE FERRET

Ferrets can also be infected by heartworm larvae from a mosquito and develop heartworm disease that mimics that in a dog. And since ferrets are becoming popular pets, the knowledge of how this disease affects them is growing broader. However, there is still much that is not understood, and heartworm disease in ferrets is still an unrecognized phenomena.

Just as in the dog, D. immitis will first show up in the distant pulmonary arteries near the surface of the lungs then migrate towards the heart. But just like in the cat, only a few worms can often cause serious health problems. Because a ferret is so small compared to the size of a full grown adult heartworm, even one worm can be hazardous. It's a mystery why the ferret can be infected at all given the speed that the heartworm ruins its own home.

The heartworms that make it into adulthood only grow about one half the size that they do in the dog. The worms can cause blood impediment on their own, and vascular lesions cause the diameters to narrow, which produces pulmonary hypertension. Ferrets seem extra susceptible to heartworm infection and vulnerable to disease produced by the presence of the worm.

Heartworm disease can cause a ferret shortness of breath and to breathe rapidly, loss of appetite, harsh breathing sounds, a bulgy appearing stomach, coughing, weakness, sluggishness and sudden death. Also, their gums could turn pale and grayish because a lack of oxygen in the blood.

Enlargements of the heart and pulmonary arteries can be seen in radiographs and is a sign of progressed heartworm disease. A blurry appearance of the lungs on a radiograph can point to lung edema. Also, their hind limbs are often weakened during the progression of the disease.

Treating ferrets that have a heartworm infection with an adulticide (kills all the heartworms fast) most often results in the death of that animal. Ferrets have a high risk of emboli because the small diameter of their blood vessels can get clogged easily.

A bi-yearly heartworm preventative for dogs called moxidectin has shown great results in ferrets. In dogs it will only prevent the infection and weaken the adult worms, but in a ferret it will slowly kill them.

Many veterinarians also give ivermectin to ferrets to kill the heartworms slowly in addition to the antibiotic doxycycline. Please be careful of doxycycline in ferrets though, they are very small and the powerful effects of doxycycline might be a lot to handle. The term “less is more” can be applied here.

HEARTWORM DISEASE IN HUMAN BEINGS

Few heartworms ever make it into adulthood in the human being. They usually cannot survive in the foreign environment of the human. However, with the increase of D. immits all over the world, it’s possible that the parasite could begin to adapt to a human’s anatomy. That is why it is important to find treatments for heartworm that it will not become resistant to.

Sometimes, after a mosquito bite, microfilariae can migrate to the lungs of a man or woman where they usually die. The lung tissue then attempts to rid itself of the foreign material and forms what is called a focal granuloma. These nodules in the lungs can sometimes cause an irritation and produce a cough.

Possibly the worst scenario that these nodules can cause is that they are sometimes mistaken for lung cancer tissue by a medical doctor after looking at them on a radiograph. The doctor will surgically open the person's chest and cut into the lungs to remove the lesion only to discover it is not what it appears to be. This can be a very dangerous surgery, so it is a good idea to protect yourself from mosquito bites. Also, if a doctor tells you that they have seen lesions on your chest x-ray and wants to perform surgery to remove them please get a second opinion.

Rarely, immature heartworms can infect the pleural space in the eye of a human being. These can be removed surgically and usually do not cause lasting damage to the eye.

Heartworms can also cause humans emotional and financial strain. I hope this book will increase people's understanding of the parasite which will lessen the negative impact on both an animal's and a human being's overall well being.

HEARTWORM DISEASE IN OTHER ANIMALS

Little is known about how D. immitis affects other animals and in how many species it can cause disease. But what has been studied shows that in most species, heartworm infection will be of a short duration and any symptoms will be self limiting and will usually be resolved by the body's self healing attributes.

WHEN HEARTWORMS DIE

Although the lesions in the pulmonary arteries initiated by adult heartworms are serious, the death of a heartworm in a host's body causes much more damage. This process begins when the worm dies and the loss of its protective coat initiates a chain of events starting with an inflammatory reaction.

When a heartworm dies its once structured form becomes soft and pulpy, turns transparent and loses its rigidity. When they are alive the worms hang around the larger pulmonary arteries. But when they die they get carried back into the far edges of the distant arteries near the surface of the lungs. Once there the body begins to break them down and the insides of the heartworm become exposed.

As the heartworm decays, it spills out the organism called Wolbachia that live in its body. It has recently been discovered that the discharged Wolbachia cause much of the inflammatory reaction inside the arteries. This discovery correlates with the new treatment protocols that call for the elimination of the Wolbachia while the heartworms are still alive. This causes the sterility of the females, and since heartworms cannot function without Wolbachia, they die. And since the Wolbachia has already been eliminated, the inflammatory reaction is lessened. This is especially important for cats and ferrets.

As the body tries to eliminate the disintegrating worm, clotting factors become activated and thrombosis (blood clotting) becomes massive. This can produce full blockages of the blood vessels which causes the oxygen starved tissue on the other side to die.

In other places the inflammatory reaction is so great that the dead and decaying heartworm becomes partially calcified and merges into the arterial wall within the scar tissue. This also creates blockages and the pulmonary pressure can skyrocket.

The body of a dog will most likely be able to cope with the natural death of a couple worms at a time. However, when a adulticide treatment is administered to an animal which is designed to kill all the heartworms at once, massive blockages and death of the tissue can produce the worst and most severe effects of heartworm disease of all.

WHAT IT ALL BOILS DOWN TO

The disease that heartworms can produce in its host can also be called endotheliitis. This is an immune response within the interior of the blood vessels causing inflammation and the gradual narrowing of the space within.

This gradual narrowing of the arteries increases the work load of the heart as it tries to pump blood to oxygenate the body. As the pulmonary pressure rises the natural functioning of the body becomes distorted. Eventually the heart could succumb to congestive heart failure as the pressure against its output proves to be too much for it.

One cause of death in a human being is endotheliitis, which can come from many disease factors. Most often endotheliitis is produced from the immense number of microscopic pathogens that circulate in the blood stream of every human being, and over time cause inflammation in the arteries. A good defense for endotheliitis is called allicin which is derived from garlic and is now available in a stabilized form.

Now that we know that endotheliitis is the product of D. immitis, we can go forward with confidence to discover ways to lessen its effects while eliminating it. There are many options for treatment, yet some of those have their own negative consequences. However, there are treatment options that will pose less danger to your pet.

FIVE

LOCATION, LOCATION, LOCATION

HEARTWORMS HAVE A LONG REACH, AND CAN be found infecting animals all over the globe. The most infected areas include the United States, South America, Japan, Australia and Italy. But not that long ago, the parasite could only survive in isolated areas of the world.

In North America, Dirofilaria immitis infections were confined to the southeastern regions near the coast line. And in Europe, infections usually occurred in the southern countries of Portugal, Spain, France, Italy, Slovenia, Bulgaria, Romania, Greece and Turkey.

Now, heartworm is found in all 50 states in America and are becoming more common even in far northern Europe such as Serbia and Croatia. Infections are also being recorded in Canada and as far north as Alaska. Some areas of the world with the highest infection rates, such as Australia and Italy, have seen an even higher incidence of heartworm in the last few years.

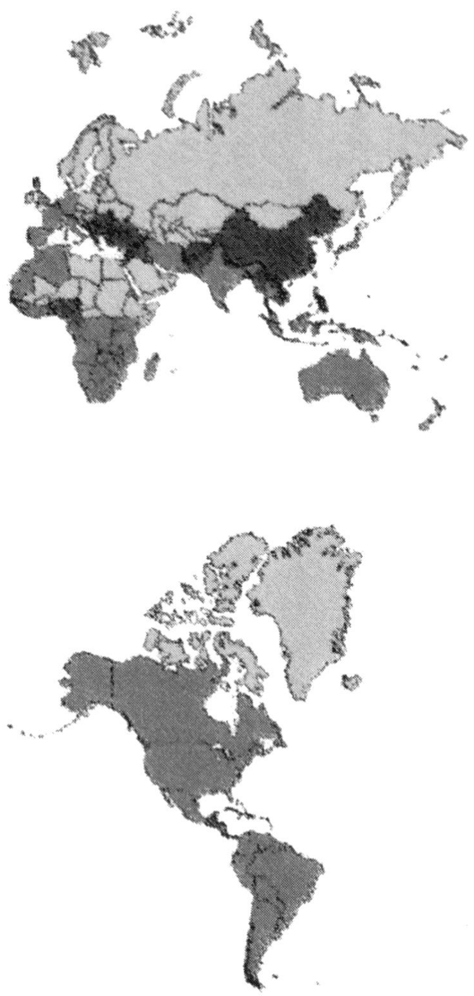

The map above represents the distribution of Dirofilaria immitis as it is today. The areas in the lighter shade, such as Greenland or Russia have a very small incidence of heartworm infections. The areas in the medium shade, such as Australia, India and Algeria have a higher incidence. And the areas in the darkest shade, such as China, Pakistan and Turkey have the highest incidence of heartworm infections.

There are many reasons why Dirofilaria immitis seems to be rapidly expanding across the globe. Globalization is making the world smaller and once isolated pockets of the world are now being exposed. In reaction, New Zealand has adopted new laws that force all dogs entering the country to be tested and treated for heartworm before they are allowed entry.

"The microfilariae that female heartworms give birth to and that circulate in the host's blood cannot grow into adults unless they are first sucked up by a mosquito and then injected back again after weeks of maturation inside the mosquito."

Chief among the spread of heartworm is the climate changes happening to our earth. Heartworms live, reproduce and spread through mosquitoes. And where there is a higher humidity and temperature there is likely to be more mosquitoes. As the planet heats up, mosquitoes and the diseases they spread radiate from the equator and march toward the poles.

There are over 3000 known species of mosquitoes that inhabit our planet. Many of these spread disease to human beings and animals. In fact, mosquitoes are considered the most dangerous animal in existence. Malaria causes more than a million deaths every year, despite efforts to minimize exposure to mosquitoes.

Mosquito-borne diseases involve transmission of parasites and viruses from animal to person, person to person and animal to animal. Some of these diseases mostly affect human beings, such as malaria and the dengue virus.

Mosquitoes also spread filarial disease as well. The nematode O. Volvulus, which spreads the disease called human river blindness, is the second leading cause of blindness to human beings. The heartworm and the increasingly dangerous French heartworm get passed around by mosquitoes. Also spread by the mosquito is the lung worm which infects both dogs and cats.

Among the many species of mosquitoes, only a handful are known to carry the larvae of Dirofilaria immitis. However, more mosquitoes are being discovered that harbor the heartworm until it is developed enough to infect a new host.

The earth has already seen an increase of its average temperature by more than one °C in the last 100 years, and global temperatures are expected to rise at least two °C by the year 2100.

Mosquitoes do not need a tropical environment to thrive. The optimal temperature for the larvae of heartworm to develop is from 22.5 °C to 26.5 °C (72.5 °F to 79.7 °F). Below 14 °C (57.2 °F) the heartworm larvae will become dormant until the temperate rises again.

The reason for global warming is debatable, but the fact remains that the earth's temperature is rising. This will increase the likelihood that mosquito-borne pathogens will be on the rise as well.

PREVENTION FIRST

If you live in or travel through any of the areas where mosquitoes spread heartworm your pets are in danger. Even passing through an area endemic for heartworm puts them at risk. Preventing mosquito bites is the first line of defense.

Keeping mosquitoes away from ourselves and our pets is the principle action that we can take to prevent infection. One mosquito can only transmit a few heartworm larvae in a single bite. And the larvae will have to have some luck surviving the animals immune system, especially if it is strong.

It's important to understand that only the larvae that a mosquito injects are able to grow into adults. The microfilariae that female heartworms give birth to and that circulate in the host's blood cannot grow into adults unless they are first sucked up by a mosquito and then injected back again after weeks of maturation inside the mosquito.

"Keeping mosquitoes away from ourselves and our pets is the principle action that we can take to prevent infection."

Mosquito Control

In this section we will discuss ways of minimizing mosquitoes around you, your family and your pets. You do not have to do all these things, just pick the ones that come easiest to you. Unless you have a serious mosquito problem, employing just a couple of the methods in this section should reduce chances of being bit.

Mosquito control can pose dangers as well. There are products and chemicals out there that do more harm than good. We can take away a good lesson by learning a little history about a well known insecticide called DDT.

DDT is now banned in most of the world. Maybe you have seen the videos of children being blanketed with the fog of DDT while loudly proclaiming its harmlessness in the 1960's. Not too long after this it was revealed that DDT causes cancer, birth defects and a myriad of other tragic health defects in animals and human beings.

All the while DDT was poisoning the world in the name of protecting it, an undercurrent of politics raged on. The struggle between those that seek profit and those that want to protect the environment is still being waged. What side do you think is winning?

Although DDT saved countless lives from malaria, its efficiency has lost its edge. Many mosquitoes are now resistant to the effects. Resistance to man made chemicals is normal in nature.

The best approach to mosquito control is to not wage war on nature, but to intelligently apply those things it has already given us. If we use the chemicals they keep giving us then they will eventually become useless and we will need another. All the while the environment becomes unbalanced and they profit from it.

So let's begin by not harming the creatures in our own yards that are the mosquitoes' natural enemies. Living things such as bats, birds, fish, insects, spiders, bacteria, fungus, frogs and lizards all reduce the mosquito population.

Bats feed exclusively on insects and one bat can easily eat more than 1000 mosquitoes a hour! Few bats carry rabies and very few human beings have caught the disease from them. Contrary to popular belief, bats are friendly and extremely beneficial to human beings.

A bat house is a simple structure that can be a home to bats. Each bat will eat thousands of bugs and mosquitoes on your property every day. You can build one yourself or purchase one. Type in "bat house" online and you will find many results.

Have you ever spent evenings outside under the hum and glow of a bug zapper? If you have you will remember the sound of insects being electrocuted. Bug zappers are actually not effective against mosquitoes, unless there are additional ways built in to attract them. They also kill the beneficial bugs that eat mosquitoes. So a bug zapper will only increase the mosquito population. Also, when a bug is electrocuted they explode sending a fine mist of bacteria and viruses many feet around the zapper.

Since most insecticides kill the natural predators of mosquitoes, an intelligent choice is to use only the natural ones. Studies have shown that after a decade of insecticide spraying, the mosquito population increased 15 times. Insecticides can also lower the immune systems of animals and humans making the entire ecosystem more vulnerable to disease, including some carried by mosquitoes.

Insecticides kill fish, birds and disrupt the natural rhythms of the natural environment. The weaker the body of the living creature, the more susceptible they are. It seems foolish to use toxic insecticides except during extreme infestation.

If you need to spray your yard, use products that contain Bacillus thuringiensis, a natural insecticide. There are also lawn sprays made out of garlic concentrate, but might not be effective on all mosquito species.

The best defense against mosquitoes is removing any standing water around your home. Stagnant water is where mosquitoes hatch their young. Without it, you will see a huge impact on the mosquito population around your property.

Walk around the outside of your house with the purpose of spotting any standing water. Look for:

- Old tires
- Buckets
- Leaking faucets
- Clogged gutters
- Plastic swimming pools
- Tree stumps, puddles
- Lawn furniture
- Toys

Change the water frequently in bird baths, empty any plastic swimming pools when they are not in use and fill or drain any holes. Diatomaceous earth, an ultra fine powder, can be lightly dusted over any mud or wet areas on the ground or lawn but be careful to not breathe it.

Treat permanent swimming pools and keep your pump and filter systems running. Koi ponds, hydroponic systems, animal water troughs, bird baths, rain barrels and any other pools of water can be treated with mosquito dunks made with Bacillus thuringiensis.

You can also look up your city's website for "mosquito control." Many cities are now offering free guppy like fish called mosquito fish (Gambusia affinis) that eat mosquito larvae in water. They can be used in watering troughs, ditches, ornamental ponds and anywhere that holds water. You will only need a few of them because they breed easily and multiply fast. They should not be released into the natural ecosystem as they can cause harm and imbalance.

Make sure to keep your lawn mowed and try to eliminate any weedy areas. Sprinkle a fine layer of diatomaceous earth over dirt in any potted plants, flowers or trees. This will keep mosquitoes and other bugs out and will not affect the pH.

Many plants, flowers, herbs and trees are natural mosquito deterrents. Place these around your home, especially where you sit outside and near entrances. They will help repel mosquitoes and add ambience to your home. I especially love sassafras and neem trees.

Mosquitoes are not strong flyers, so fans are great for keeping them away. Place a fan so it blows air across entrances from outside, and at night place a fan so air blows across the room where you and your pets sleep.

Also, install screens on windows and repair any holes or gaps in the existing screens. If you leave a door open to the outside for your pet to go in and out of the house you can install a screen mesh in the entrance. Type in the keywords "mosquito curtains" online.

NATURAL MOSQUITO DETERRENTS:

- Rose-scent geranium (Pelargonium graveolens)
- Lemon balm (Melissa officinalis)
- Neem tree (Azadirachta indica)
- Sassafras tree (Sassafras albidum)
- Catnip (Nepeta cataria)
- Basil (Ocimum basilicum)
- Horsemint (Mentha longifolia)
- Lemon eucalyptus (Corymbia citriodora)
- Rosemary (Rosmarinus officinalis)
- Lavender (Lavandula angustifolia)
- Marigold (Calendula officinalis)
- Citronella (Cymbopogon)
- Sage (Salvia officinalis)

Replace all light bulbs near the entrances of your home with non-attractive bulbs. LED and sodium vapor bulbs do not attract mosquitoes. Chances are your existing bulbs bring a swarm of insects that circle around the light until they decide to enter your home.

You can also burn mosquito repelling candles outside and in your home. Most of these contain citronella, but more gentle ones can also contain clove and lavender. Also, mosquito coils are effective, cheap and easily attainable.

There are many ways of making simple mosquito traps that trap or kill the mosquitoes inside. The Internet has many examples and videos which you can find by typing in "mosquito traps."

Mosquitoes are attracted to the carbon dioxide in exhaled breath and the odor emanating from the skin in mammals, which includes you and your pets. When you go outside with your pets in the summer, chances are mosquitoes will be drawn to you. It's great to know how to repel mosquitoes safely from you and your pets when you go outdoors. Remember, only the mosquito can transmit heartworm.

Place the mosquito repelling plants and trees all around the area that you and your pets spend time. Try to not leave your pets outside before dawn and after dusk since that is when the mosquitoes are most active. You can also apply mosquito repellent to your body. But be very careful if you apply anything to your animal's fur as it can be toxic to them.

Animals will lick their fur and ingest whatever they clean off of it. Cats and ferrets are more sensitive than dogs, and mosquito repellent can prove deadly to them.

First off, please do not ever apply any products containing DEET to your pets. This is toxic if ingested, and just because it is approved for human beings by the Center of Disease Control and Prevention in the United States doesn't mean its safe. We now understand that most of the products promoted by the major governments are huge money makers for vested interests. Spraying it on our bodies is bad enough, but extremely dangerous if ingested like an animal will do when it cleans itself.

Also watch out for products containing lemon eucalyptus which is also approved by the Center of Disease Control and Prevention in the United States for mosquito control. The products that contain this also put buffers in the ingredients that are not listed on the bottle. Even though lemon eucalyptus is natural, it is not safe for animals and that is clearly stated on all the manufacturer's websites.

The most gentle and effective body mosquito repellents are made with gentle essential oils of neem, citronella, lavender and rose geranium. These can be used alone or mixed however you wish. Mix one teaspoon of the essential oil with one cup (8 ounces) of soybean oil or olive oil. Dab a tiny amount on the back of your dog's neck which they will have a hard time licking.

A better option would be to only apply the oil to your own body, which will help keep the mosquitoes away from your pets as well. Remember that dogs have a keen sense of smell which can prove to be overwhelming to them. Also, never apply any essential oils to a cat's or ferret's body which can be poisonous to them.

OTHER PREVENTATIVES

The second most important prevention of heartworm infection is the health of your animal. Every living thing has an immune system, and when it is running efficiently, provides some protection against intruders.

However, when an animal's health is compromised, invaders have a much better chance of getting inside. Nutrition is a debatable subject, and there are many who say one thing and some who say another. But fresh foods are always best. Fresh vegetables, meat, lentils and oatmeal is a cheap but healthy diet.

A healthy animal will always be one that is given love and attention in abundance. Care and love trumps any other health giving substance twofold. Playing and spending time with that animal strengthens its immune system, and floods good chemicals and feelings through its body. Spending time in nature in the fresh air and sunshine will bring immense benefits to both you and your pets.

Be careful of over vaccinating your pets. There is evidence that too many vaccinations can weaken your pet's immune system and make them vulnerable to many other diseases and pathogens. There are many good resources and books online about the subject.

Give your animals fresh water every day, especially when the outdoor temperature is high. Filter your water from the tap if possible, just remember that most filters do not remove fluoride. If you live in a country that fluorinates the water supply buy bottled water (make sure it is also not fluorinated) or use reverse osmosis or distillation devices. If you cannot get pure water just make sure that they always have enough fresh water at all times, especially if they are on any medication or heartworm treatment.

PRESCRIPTION PREVENTATIVES

Lab created chemicals have been used as preventatives for heartworm infection for a long time. In the 1940's a piperazine deriative called Diethylearbamazine citrate or DEC for short was invented as a filaricide dewormer. It has been used as a treatment of filariasis in both humans and animals.

"Remember, only the mosquito can transmit heartworm."

DEC became popular in the 1970's for preventing infection of heartworms in dogs but has given way to the more potent macrocyclic lactones. Although DEC has a low toxicity, it can be extremely dangerous if given to dogs with an existing heartworm infection and circulating microfilariae. Dogs would always need to be tested for heartworm before given DEC to avoid complications. Even then there was no guarantee that the test results were accurate.

Another problem was that DEC would need to be given every single day to be effective. If the dog owner forgot just one day, it could make the dog susceptible to a heartworm infection.

If you live in or travel through any of the areas on the map that are endemic for Dirofilaria immitis, your pet has a chance to become infected. It might be wise to give them some sort of preventative.

The problem with chemical preventatives is that nature is more prone to side step them. Resistance to over the counter heartworm medication is already a reality. A mutation of Dirofilaria immitis has been found along the Mississippi river that is resistant to chemical heartworm preventatives.

Although it seems isolated to this area for now, this mutation is expected to increase. If you were to do serious research about the overall resistance of pathogens to man made chemicals you will see a pattern or trend emerge. Many world scientists are increasingly becoming alarmed at the rate that resistant viruses and parasites are killing human beings.

Another thing to be aware of is the possibility that over time, chemical preventatives will lower the immune system of an animal making them more susceptible to a parasite infection. It might be worth looking into natural heartworm preventatives as long as you test for heartworm disease in your pet at least once a year.

There are many "natural" heartworm preventatives that people talk about online and in books. But some of these can also be dangerous. Herbs like wormwood have been used for centuries to clear intestinal parasites, not those in the blood. These natural dewormers can really tax your pet's liver and kidneys, and should be used with much caution. There are much better natural preventative options available.

Most of the over-the-counter heartworm preventatives are macrocyclic lactones called avermectins that possess potent insecticidal properties. They all kill microfilariae in the blood, however they each have characteristics of their own. They are semi-natural compounds produced by fermentation of the bacteria Streptomyces avermitilis.

Some of the avermectins kill Dirofilaria immitis microfilariae very quickly, making it more likely the animal will suffer from shock to a greater or lesser degree. This can be dangerous for an animal with high amounts of microfilariae swimming around in its blood. This is the justification veterinarians give for not prescribing heartworm medication until a heartworm test has been given.

"The moment you begin giving ivermectin to your pet a heartworm infection will be prevented and any existing infection will begin being treated."

Here's some good news: ivermectin is an avermectin found in some of the major heartworm preventatives that kills the microfilariae more slowly, making the likelihood of shock less probable. Ivermectin is also part of the new protocol for heartworm treatment.

Ivermectin is used all around the world to treat many parasites. Large amounts of the drug are donated to poorer countries to fight river blindness caused by the nematode Onchocerca volvulus.

Ivermectin is a combination of macrocyclic lactones that is very effective against many types of parasites but not fungi or bacteria. It is effective in preventing heartworm infection by killing microfilariae even in minuscule amounts.

In addition to killing the microfilariae, ivermectin will suppress the reproduction of female heartworms. This puts to rest the concern that giving ivermectin to a heartworm positive dog might produce an occult infection. Since ivermectin suppresses microfilariae from being born in the first place, they will not die in the lung capillaries causing disease.

Since ivermectin kills microfilariae more slowly, there is little concern that it will produce shock in an animal. As long as ivermectin is used, a test to find out if the animal is heartworm positive first is not that important. The moment you begin giving ivermectin to your pet a heartworm infection will be prevented and any existing infection will begin being treated.

However, it would be wise to test cats and ferrets for a heartworm infection before ivermectin is given to them. Since the death of an adult heartworm can be fatal in a cat or ferret, using ivermectin can be dangerous since it hastens the heartworm's death. In other words, do not give a cat or ferret ivermectin that is heartworm positive until supportive measures are given such as reducing the inflammation inside the arteries around the adult heartworms.

There is concern that ivermectin can cause severe reactions in collies and some other breeds and mixed breeds of dogs due to a mutant MDR1 gene. The gene allows chemicals easy access across the blood–brain barrier which can cause toxicity in the animal quickly. Dogs with white feet tend to have this mutant gene as well.

The idea that the low dose for treating heartworm (6 micrograms per kilogram) is dangerous for dogs with the mutant MDR1 gene has now been proven to be false. The real danger is in the higher doses of ivermectin (300-600 micrograms per kilogram) which are used for treating diseases like mange. This is not to say that low doses of ivermectin are without any risks. Any drug should be given cautiously.

"Since the death of an adult heartworm can be fatal in a cat or ferret, using ivermectin can be dangerous since it hastens the heartworm's death."

I cannot recommend to you that you use a chemical preventative such as ivermectin because there are no guarantees of a desired outcome. Your pet could be that one in a million that reacts badly. But the low dose of ivermectin used in heartworm prevention and treatment is so small that toxicity is minimal.

Another big benefit of ivermectin is that it is easily obtainable and extremely affordable. Although it is costly when it is purchased as an over-the-counter prescription heartworm preventative, it can literally prevent heartworm in thousands of dogs, cats and ferrets if purchased cheaply in other forms.

There are a few options for acquiring ivermectin. You can go to a veterinarian which is the most costly route. They will want to give a heartworm test before prescribing it to you. But you can save money by opting for the generic version of the preventative which is made by the same manufacture. Getting ivermectin this way has the benefit of being in the form of a delicious treat that your pet will love to eat.

Also, if you decide to buy the ivermectin sold by the veterinarian, please be aware that all the brands have an option to get extra medications added into the ivermectin treats. However, this cocktail can prove to be dangerous because it is unclear how the pet will react to the mixture of drugs. It is much more wise to opt-out of the "plus" or "extra" versions of the ivermectin treats.

Some people recommend saving money by purchasing the larger doses of the prescription preventative for bigger animals and dividing them. However, you should be aware that the manufacturer has stated that the ivermectin is not evenly distributed in the edible biscuit. Even so, the variation is probably small.

If you are on a budget or wish to avoid the veterinarian's office you can purchase a 1% ivermectin solution and dilute it to dose your pet yourself. This is perfect for animal shelters or people that have a large amount of pets in their care or just cannot afford the expensive veterinarian visit.

There are many stories online about animals being euthanized because they had a heartworm infection and the shelter could not afford treatment. Since ivermectin can be bought for pennies a dose, and can be used for both prevention and treatment, there is no reason any animal should be killed because a lack of funds available.

"It is much more wise to opt-out of the "plus" or "extra" versions of the ivermectin treats."

MAKING YOUR OWN PREVENTATIVE

Measuring ivermectin is not so easy because we need to portion it using micrograms. Based on the recommendations of the FDA at six micrograms per kilogram for dogs, a 50 milliliter bottle of 1% ivermectin contains enough to dose 83,333 kilograms or 183,717 pounds of dog. Or one drop will treat one 68 kilogram (150 pound) dog. At these measurements it's best to dilute it a bit.

If you decide to go this route it's important that you do the math correctly. Check and recheck your measurements. Some companies sell pre-mixed solutions of ivermectin at very affordable prices if you do not want to do it yourself. Just type in "heartworm prevention ivermectin generic" in your online search engine. However, be aware that these dilutions are usually stronger than the recommended dosages probably to ensure the efficiency of their product.

Making your own diluted ivermectin for your pet can be a lot of fun. It's also a great accomplishment because you are taking charge of your pet's health, saving a lot of money and making something worth while. So relax, make sure your measurements are right and enjoy.

First, you will need a bottle of propylene glycol or glycerine. Either one will work well as a solvent to dilute the ivermectin to a more workable volume. Both cost about the same and can be found online for under ten American dollars for a pint size bottle.

You will also need a way to measure drops and milliliters. A syringe that measures one mL/cc or more and has the metal needle so you can puncture the plastic top of the ivermectin bottle to draw out the fluid is ideal. These can be bought online or at most drug stores for only a few dollars.

Next, you will need to purchase a glass dropper bottle and eye dropper. Any size bottle of 50 mL or more will be necessary using our measurements. These can be found online, health food stores or herb stores for under a couple dollars.

Finally, you will need the bottle of ivermectin in a 1% solution. Make sure it is not a "pour on" but an "injectable." It must say that it is a 1% solution where each mL contains ten mg of ivermectin. There are a few manufacturers of the drug so you will have some choices. A 100 mL bottle of ivermectin can be found at animal feed stores and online for around $30 dollars.

It's very important that you purchase pure ivermectin and not one that has added drugs. It should be easy to spot since the label will not contain words such as "plus" or "extra." The added drugs could threaten the life of your pet because of the concentration in the liquid, so make sure you know what you are buying.

It will cost less than $50 dollars for everything needed to make thousands of heartworm preventative dosages. At this price no animal should ever be turned away because of a lack of funds for medicine.

SOME ESSENTIAL MEASUREMENTS:

- mL = milliliter
- cc = cubic centimeter
- mcg = microgram
- 1 cc = 1 mL
- 1 mL = 20 drops
- 1 drop = .05 mL
- 1 mL 1% ivermectin = 10 mg ivermectin
- 10 mg 1% ivermectin = 10,000 mcg ivermectin
- 1 drop 1% ivermectin = 500 mcg ivermectin

Place these on a clean table surface: one bottle 1% ivermectin, one bottle propylene glycol or glycerine, one small glass dropper bottle and eye dropper (pipette), and one syringe with a metal needle which can measure one mL/cc.

When performing dilutions of liquids a volume to volume is preferred over measurements using weights. We are going to make a one in 50 or 1:50 dilution to make it easier to measure the correct dosages. The mathematics are different when measuring ratios of dilutions and it is critical to understand the difference. The larger number in 1:50 is the total final volume (ivermectin + glycol or glycerine). The smaller number is the amount of the solute (ivermectin). The larger number subtracted by the smaller number makes the amount of the solvent (glycol or glycerine.) This makes a 1:50 dilution one part solute and 49 parts solvent. Many people make the mistake of making a dilution of one part solute and 50 parts solvent.

On a clean surface, place your materials in front of you. Open the dropper bottle and the bottle of glycerine or glycol. Using the syringe, draw out the glycerine or glycol and squirt it into the dropper bottle until it is 49 mL/cc full. You should make a mark on a piece of paper for every mL/cc as you go so you do not lose track.

Next, poke the needle into the bottle of 1% ivermectin and draw out one mL/cc of liquid. Now squirt the one mL/cc of 1% ivermectin into the dropper bottle containing the 49 mL/cc of glycerine or glycol. Gently swirl the liquid for a minute and then screw the eye dropper onto the dropper bottle. Shake the bottle vigorously for a minute or two and allow it to sit for 24 hours or more to allow the liquids to diffuse properly before using it.

This liquid solution of 1% ivermectin is diluted 50 times. Instead of being 500 micrograms per drop it is now ten micrograms per drop. Now it will be easy to dose both large and small animals for only pennies per animal.

Here are the recommended preventative doses by body weight for dogs and cats published by the FDA in the United States. Although these numbers have not been established for ferrets yet, most veterinarians would agree that the cat dose would be sufficient for a preventative.

- Dogs = six mcg per kilogram (2.72 mcg per pound)
- Cats/ferrets = 24 mcg per kilogram (10.9 mcg per pound)

After you know how much your pet weighs and have done the math to calculate the correct dosage you can give the preventative once a month for now on. A 35 pound dog will need 2.72 mcg per pound which is 95.2 mcg rounded down to 95 mcg. Since our dilution is ten mcg per drop we can give ten drops which will total 100 mcg rounded up. For another example, a ten pound cat needs 10.9 mcg per pound for the preventative dose of invermectin. That equals to 110 mcg rounded up or 11 drops of our dilution.

Since even small amounts of ivermectin will prevent heartworm, it is not necessary to be exact in your measurements. Just be as precise as you can. Also, it's a good idea to have a calendar that you can mark on so you will always remember the next time you need to give them the next dose.

To administer the diluted ivermectin simply put the drops onto something that you know they will have no hesitation eating. Cans of food are good for this as are foods that can absorb the drops of liquid such as bread or rice. Just make sure that they consume the entire dose.

Ivermectin dosages for heartworm prevention are very low. For example, the dosage for mange in dogs is 60 times higher than it is for heartworm prevention. Even so, watch your pet closely for the next few hours to make sure there are no adverse reactions. Keep an eye out for anything out of the ordinary such as an unsteady balance, vomiting, blindness and any other serious reaction and take them to the emergency veterinarian if necessary.

It has been theorized that not giving a chemical heartworm preventative consistently could lower its efficiency. However, it could also be possible that giving a drug without any rest or time in between might lower an animal's immune system making it more vulnerable to disease from a heartworm infection.

You will have to decide between these conflicting ideas whether or not you will give a preventative year round. You can save money and keep the animal's toxicity level to a minimum by only administering the preventative during the mosquito season. In addition, you might consider giving the animal the preventative once every 45 days instead of every 30. There is much evidence that ivermectin will still be efficient at killing all the microfilariae at this interval.

It doesn't have to be complicated trying to figure out when to start and stop the preventative. World temperature maps and graphs are not needed. Simply start when the first mosquito is seen and continue for two months after the last mosquito is seen. Do not worry, it doesn't have to be exact. Be aware however that some mosquitoes can live longer. Some concrete structures can act as urban heat islands and hold the sun's heat long enough to allow the mosquito a longer life.

Ivermectin is partially natural, derived from the fermentation of the bacteria Streptomyces avermitilis. There are also two natural medicines that show huge potential as a preventative and a treatment for heartworm infection and disease. They are black seeds from the Nigella sativa plant and stabilized allicin from garlic bulbs.

Six

Let's Get This Fixed

If an animal in your care has developed an infection of heartworm disease there is no cause to fear. There are many solutions for treating and eliminating the parasite. That light at the end of the tunnel is not a freight train.

Even though cats and ferrets are more susceptible than dogs to health problems associated with Dirofilaria immitis, there is no cause to despair either. There are also options and solutions to bring your ferret or cat back to vibrant health.

If you recently found out that your pet has a heartworm infection, you are concerned and want answers. That is why you bought this book. For every question there is an answer. So clear your mind, take a deep breath and let's proceed with a calm but resolute direction towards eliminating and healing the pet in your care.

Are You Heartworm Positive?

There are signals that an animal exhibits that hint of a positive heartworm infection.

A series of classes has been developed for dogs to give better criteria for treatment.

- Class 1: Mild or no symptoms, occasional cough.
- Class 2: Mild to moderate symptoms such as occasional cough and shortness of breath.
- Class 3: Body deterioration, tiredness after mild activity or at rest and trouble breathing.
- Class 4: Caval syndrome, sudden weakness, blood disorders and exhaustion.

Sometimes dogs will not show any symptoms until they come on all at once. Be on the look out for breathing difficulties (rapid breathing or excessive panting while at rest), a gravely cough, abnormal lung sounds and becoming easily winded after exercise.

Cats usually show no clinical signs until they come on suddenly. A sudden onset of rapid breathing, cough or death are most often the only signs a feline will exhibit that has an adult heartworm infection. Watch for persistent cough, breathing difficulties (wheezing, rapid breathing, panting, harsh lung sounds), depression, weight loss and lack of appetite, tiredness and vomiting.

Ferrets will exhibit similar clinical symptoms of a dog that has heartworm disease. They seem to be very susceptible to Dirofilaria immitis. Watch for coughing, tiredness, a puffy abdomen, trouble breathing and pale areas around the mouth. In addition, their urine can turn a shade of green.

It can be distressing to see an animal you love showing any of these symptoms. There might be other underlying health issues that are causing the symptoms other then heartworm disease. Either way, it might be wise to get them medical attention as soon as possible.

If you live in an area on the map that is endemic for heartworm infection and your pet is exhibiting any symptoms or just not feeling good, it is probably wise to get a heartworm test as well.

TESTING, TESTING, 1..2..3

If you have ever taken your dog to the veterinarian's office they probably suggested a heartworm test to find out if he or she has an infection. This is especially important for cats and ferrets, since eliminating any heartworms can be dangerous for them.

Heartworm tests evolved in the 1980's specifically because it was so dangerous to give the preventative called DEC (diethylcarbamazine) to an animal with circulating microfilariae. Remember, this compound could cause serious health problems for a heartworm positive animal.

DEC is rarely used anymore for heartworm prevention since it was replaced by the more reliable avermectins. However, heartworm tests are still mandatory for pet owners before an avermectin preventative will even be sold to them.

But, it is valuable to know whether a sick canine has a heartworm infection so they can be treated. Or, if you would rather spare the dog monthly doses of preventative, you might opt to do bi-yearly or yearly heartworm tests instead. If the dog was suddenly to test positive for heartworm, you could just start giving them ivermectin monthly.

There are a few types of heartworm tests: antigen, antibody and microfilariae detection. Antigen tests are currently the most popular for dogs, as they are the most accurate. However, they only detect female worms and are not very accurate when there are less than 3 of them or are immature.

An antigen test detects foreign proteins circulating in the blood that are produced by female heartworms. A small amount of blood will be needed from your pet. Heartworm antigen test kits are manufactured by many companies. The tests are easy to perform and quick to show results. You can order your own antigen test kits if you wish, just type in "heartworm antigen test kit" in your browser.

Veterinarians routinely tell their customers that antigen tests are always accurate, but the reality is that they often produce false negatives and sometimes false positives. That is why it is important to do a follow up test if the animal does test positive.

Antibody tests are often used to test for a heartworm infection in a cat or ferret because they very sensitive. It can detect a very small infection, which is perfect for a small animal. However, it can't detect whether a cat or ferret has an active infection or was only exposed to the heartworm and successfully fought off the intruder. Because of this they are prone to produce false positives.

Detecting microfilariae in the blood is another way to test for Dirofilaria immitis, however this method is not very dependable. Remember, microfilariae might not be present in animals with an occult infection, sterilized females, older worms or an all male or all female infection. But they can be used as a second indicator after an animal has tested positive for heartworm from another test.

Back when DEC was the only available preventative, microfilariae tests were most often given before DEC was provided. But given the unreliability of these tests, I wonder how many adverse reactions to DEC there were when it was prescribed to dogs with an active infection.

"If the dog was suddenly to test positive for heartworm, you could just start giving them ivermectin monthly."

If your pet does test positive for heartworm infection you might want to get other confirming evidence that an infection does indeed exist. In most cases a chest x-ray and a microfilariae test will be all that's needed to confirm the test results. Sometimes an electrocardiogram can used to detect evidence of right ventricular hypertrophy caused from an elevated blood pressure.

IT'S POSITIVE, NOW WHAT?!

I know what it feels like to find out that an animal you love has heartworm disease. But I bet it would make you feel better to know that as soon as treatment is begun, the animal will start to improve. Although an active heartworm infection will harm the internals of an animal, the day that treatment is begun the damage will begin to heal.

You need to decide how you intend to treat the infected animal, if at all. There are many choices ahead of you that will be competing for you attention. Indeed, heartworm disease is a convoluted subject, and you will have to discern the right way to go which will not always be clear. But let go of your doubt and fear, relax and trust in the resilience of your pet.

The veterinarian that administered the test will want to treat your pet. But first they will want to perform what's called a "pretreatment evaluation." They do this to determine which symptoms need to be stabilized before the actual treatment to eliminate the heartworms begins.

The pretreatment evaluation uses an algorithm to plan the best ways to treat the animal. It seeks to avoid complications from toxic drugs and embolisms that form when the heartworms die in mass amounts. First, information will collected and compiled into what is called a minimum data base abbreviated as MDB.

The MDB will be tailored to the animal's geographic area, age and clinical symptoms. It can inlcude:

- History
- Physical evaluation
- Thoracic x-ray
- Complete blood count
- Electrocardiogram
- Urinalysis
- Serum urea nitrogen level

Once the MDB has been compiled your veterinarian will layout the plan for treating and eliminating heartworms from your pet after any other health problems have been stabilized. After hearing the treatment options you will have to decide for yourself if they are worth the risk to your pet.

TREATMENT OPTIONS

Currently there is no official treatment for cats and ferrets with heartworm disease. So far the medical complex has not unrolled their approved plan for these animals. However, there are good alternative options available which we will discuss shortly.

> "But let go of your doubt and fear, relax and trust in the resilience of your pet."

For decades the primary treatment for heartworm disease in a dog was to eliminate the heartworms from the dog's body using a toxic arsenic compound that would initiate the death of all the worms at once. At the same time the elimination of all microfilariae using a anthelmintic compound would be employed.

The rationale for this radical approach to quickly rid the animal of all heartworms and their microfilariae originated in the 1940's. Unfortunately, the drug called thiacetarsamide that they used to kill the heartworms also killed a large percentage of dogs. Despite the dismal record of the drug, the rationale that this was the only way to treat a heartworm infection became cemented into mainstream veterinarian medicine for almost a century.

Amazingly this is still the preferred protocol worldwide for treating dogs infected with Dirofilaria immitis. Probably the method became gospel because of a lack of other successful treatment options. In most countries, the drug thiacetarsamide has been replaced with a bit less insidious drug called melarsomine dihydrochloride.

Melarsomine is marketed as Immiticide® by a huge drug manufacturer called Merial. Just like the drugs used before it Melarsomine is considered an adulticide. An adulticide is any compound or group of compounds that act directly against parasitic organisms. Adulticides can be powerful and dangerous, and it is not by chance that adulticide sounds like cyanide.

Melarsomine is extremely toxic and must be given intravenously. If only a small amount gets on a dog's tissue, a painful lesion can develop. The toxicity of the compound is its first dangerous effects. It is very important to monitor a dog closely for adverse reactions when this is administered. Some dogs have died because their bodies could not cope with the toxic properties of the drug.

The second way that melarsomine can produce life threatening effects in a dog lies in its function of initiating the deaths of all the heartworms at once. Once the worms die it can take more than 40 days for them to turn into a soft pulpy mass. These dead heartworm fragments can persist until the dog's body can absorb them. Until then the large amount of decaying heartworms will produce massive amounts of embolisms inside the pulmonary arteries. These embolic showers initiate a inflammatory response that can be so chronic that the decaying heartworms get absorbed into the arterial wall while becoming partially calcified.

Before a heartworm dies a protective coat protects it from the host's immune system. But after its death this protective coating dissolves spilling the insides of the worm into the canal of the artery. The symbiotic bacteria Wolbachia also becomes exposed to the body's immune system creating an avalanche of inflammation as the body tries to repair itself.

As the inflammation produces further narrowing of the arteries all over the body, a sudden increase in arterial pressure can put a huge work load on the already weakened heart. This unexpected resistance against the flow of the blood from the heart could provoke the onset of right sided congestive heart failure. It's also not uncommon for dogs to begin coughing blood after receiving the drug. Blood becomes spread throughout the airways producing further inflammation.

Arsenic based adulticides like melarsomine and thiacetarsamide can also induce liver and kidney failure. In addition, the toxic drugs can also mimic the effects of an awful condition called disseminated intravascular coagulopathy. This is a condition that produces uncontrolled blood clotting inside all the blood vessels of the body. As the blood platelets are used up, abnormal bleeding occurs from the skin and many other areas.

Normally, this pathology is reserved for those that are critically ill or suffering from septic shock, massive burns or poisoning. But it is common for dogs that receive a arsenic based adulticide to suffer from this to a degree as well. Most dogs will recover from this massive injury to their entire body, but regretfully some won't be so lucky.

After understanding the impact that a drug like melarsomine has on a dog's body, anyone with even a little common sense would wonder if the effects of the drug are actually worse then the disease it seeks to cure. Although we are not in the dark ages of medicine anymore, most veterinarians treat heartworm disease as if we still were.

Arsenic based adulticides should never be used in cats and ferrets to treat heartworm disease. These drugs will kill them with the probability of a flip of a coin. Most veterinarians have learned this already and will not attempt to treat your cat or ferret with those drugs.

Interestingly, in September of 2011 Merial sent out letters to veterinarians informing them that their drug melarsomine dihydrochloride would soon be running out due to technical issues in the manufacturing process. This caused much confusion in pet owners, veterinarians and animal shelters worldwide. In some cases animal shelters began to euthanize dogs that arrived infected with heartworms believing that there was no treatment available. Sounds unbelievable doesn't it?

Since then melarsomine has become intermittently available again to veterinarians for use in treating heartworm disease. If you are pressured by your veterinarian to give an arsenic based adulticide to your dog please don't allow them to bully you or guilt trip you into using it. Whether it is melarsomine dihydrochloride or thiacetarsamide sodium (still used in some countries and marketed under the name Caparsolate®) please be aware that post-adulticide complications are very real.

This is not to say that some dogs won't benefit from the arsenic based adulticides. There are just to many variables to say that all dogs should not be treated with them. It could be that in your dog's situation they will be served best by eliminating heartworms from their body using the drugs. But, in light of the massive damage caused by the adulticides, deciding to use them in your dog should be weighed with much thought and consideration before you commit to such a serious decision.

If you do decide in favor of the arsenic drug there are some ways that you can lessen its negative impact. It was recently discovered that using a antibiotic called doxycycline before administering the adulticide will considerably lessen the damage caused by the resulting embolisms. The doxycycline will destroy the Wolbachia living inside the heartworms before they can become exposed to the body's defenses greatly lessening the inflammation that would result otherwise. You can insist on this treatment even if you are not given the option. Also, dogs should always be given a probiotic when taking doxycycline to replace the good bacteria in their gut.

Aspirin will also lessen the damage caused by the dying heartworms. The aspirin will reduce the inflammation and keep the platelets in the blood from building up which make the arteries more narrow and increase blood pressure. Just be sure to inform your veterinarian to insure there are no negative drug interactions.

IN WITH THE NEW, OUT WITH THE OLD

Fortunately, the gap when melarsomine was unavailable opened up new and better ways to treat heartworm disease in dogs. Animal medicine has at least acknowledged some of the recent advances in heartworm treatment that have come to light.

In fact, the monumental discovery of the essential role that Wolbachia bacteria play in the functioning and survival of Dirofilaira immitis has opened up a totally new and radical approach to treating the infection. It was discovered that eliminating the Wolbachia in a heartworm would first make it sterile and unable to reproduce, and then deprive it of essential molecules needed for the functioning of its body.

Also, eliminating the Wolbachia before the heartworm dies will lessen the damage produced after they die and decompose. The embolisms that form around the dead heartworms will not be as severe had the Wolbachia been exposed to the interior arteries. This is especially significant in cats and ferrets, who could possibly die because of the death of just one heartworm. There's also evidence that Wolbachia is partly responsible for Heartworm Associated Respiratory Disease (HARD) in cats.

We can now approach eliminating an active infection of Dirofilaria immitis the same way we would with lyme disease. Instead of focusing all our attention on killing the heartworm directly, it's now possible to target the symbiotic Wolbachia that live within the heartworm. This effectively makes barren the female heartworms and freezes the mechanisms that make their body function properly.

Lyme disease is caused by at least 3 species of bacteria belonging to the genus Borrelia. Because Wolbachia bacteria are similar to Borrelia in many ways they can be eliminated using similar methods. The challenge is in finding the right compounds that effectively penetrate and kill the bacteria with a minimal or zero toxicity to the host.

> "In fact, the monumental discovery of the essential role that Wolbachia bacteria play in the functioning and survival of Dirofilaira immitis has opened up a totally new and radical approach to treating the infection."

For now, it is becoming a more common practice in the veterinarian's office to use an antibiotic called doxycycline to kill the Wolbachia living inside the heartworms. Doxycycline is one in a group of antibiotics called tetracyclines. In combination with other drugs, this antibiotic is also used to treat Lyme disease.

Even though doxycycline seems to be very efficient at killing the Wolbachia bacteria it also has its limitations. For instance, organisms can mutate around antibiotics more easily than they can other compounds meant to destroy them. Bacteria are amazingly resilient and ingenious in side stepping threats to their survival. Over time, it could happen that Wolbachia will become resistant to doxycycline. That is why it is important to discover and research new and better ways in dealing with these bacteria.

Also, doxycycline can cause an already sick animal to become weaker as it copes with the heavy effects of the drug. Overall, doxycycline is quite safe. However, it should be used with caution while observing for serious side effects. Weakness, vomiting and a hypersensitivity to the sun are common symptoms.

Make sure and give your animal lots of water and keep them inside and out of the sun since their eyes and skin will be very sensitive to sunlight. Doxycycline will also kill the good bacteria living in the bowels so it is important to give them a probiotic supplement to replenish them. It's ok to give food to the animal first which will lessen stomach upset but will not alter the effects of the the drug.

Doxycycline is very good at attacking a heartworm infection. In fact, it could theoretically be used alone as the sole treatment since it does exactly what we want it to do. Doxycycline reduces risk of embolism, weakens and kills the adult and immature heartworms slowly, and makes the females barren and unable to reproduce. It also destroys migrating tissue-phase larvae and restricts microfilariae production.

The American Heartworm Society recommends giving doxycycline to dogs at 10mg/kg twice a day for 4 weeks. However, other lab studies have shown that 10mg/kg once a day is quite effective. Since doxycycline is very soluble in fat, its effects will build up over time. Because of this it seems fair to say that the "less is more" philosophy holds true for doxycycline use.

It's important that the drug stay in the blood long enough to destroy the Wolbachia that live inside the heartworm. That is why it is good to give doxycycline for an extended amount of time versus intermittently. 30 days seems like an effective duration to administer the drug. More than this can weaken the animal more than necessary. This length of time should also be long enough to sterilize and initiate the death of most of the heartworms and microfilariae.

The new treatment protocol also recommends giving a monthly preventative dose of ivermectin to dogs in conjunction with the doxycycline. This combination works together synergistically to slowly eliminate the heartworm and larvae. Time will probably prove that killing the heartworms slowly versus killing them fast is the safest and best route to take. Yes, the heartworms cause damage while still alive. But they cause much more damage when they die, especially all at once.

It seems that the period of time when melarsomine (Immiticide®) was not available has opened up some breathing room to discover new and better ways to eliminate heartworms from a host. If the adulticide melarsomine continued to stay on the shelves there is a good chance that any progress would be stifled by those who control the market.

WHAT ABOUT CATS AND FERRETS?

If you have a cat or ferret that has tested positive for a heartworm infection, chances are you feel helpless and unsure what to do. The reason for this is there are very few studies that shed any light on this disease in cats and ferrets. Even though there is a growing body of knowledge about a cat's or ferret's relationship with heartworms, the authorities seem reluctant or not prepared to authorize any treatment.

We already know that adulticides such as melarsomine will kill a large percentage of cats and ferrets if given the drug. Melarsomine will kill the heartworms just as it does in dogs. However, the death of even one heartworm can prove to be disastrous in a cat or ferret. There is a high risk of sudden death from an embolism because of the small diameter of blood vessels that can get clogged easily.

Surgery to remove the heartworms is an option but can prove to be difficult, especially in ferrets. Another route to take is to just allow the heartworms to live, while treating any symptoms and lessening inflammation with a drug called prednisone.

There are some recent studies which are trying to determine if doxycycline will lessen the damage that occurs when heartworms die sufficient enough to not kill a cat. We already know that doxycycline works well in dogs by eliminating Wolbachia bacteria which cause much of the damage when they are released when the worms die. Theoretically, this should also work in cats and ferrets. However, the saying "less is more" should definitely be applied to doxycycline especially in small animals. Doxycycline might prove to be one of the best ways to treat a heartworm infection in a cat or ferret.

There has also been some hopeful results using a drug called moxidectin in ferrets. Moxidectin is an avermectin similar to ivermectin which are produced by the fermentation of the bacteria Streptomyces avermitilis. Apparently, moxidectin will kill the heartworms slowly enough to not put the ferrets life in jeopardy. Many ferrets have already been treated this way with very high results of success.

If you would like to treat your ferret's heartworm infection using moxidectin, find a veterinarian that has some knowledge about this and is willing to try it. The veterinarian should have no problem acquiring the moxidectin under the new Minor Use Minor Species Act (MUMS) in the United States. Moxidectin should also be available worldwide in many parasite control medications for pets.

Moxidectin might also work to treat a heartworm infection in cats. It has been shown in the laboratory that cats with an existing heartworm infection tolerated moxidectin without complications. If moxidectin were to be given to cats infected with heartworms it is possible that the drug would kill the heartworm slowly enough to not put the cat's life in jeopardy. Coupled with doxycycline in small quantities, this treatment might prove to work.

Cat's could also be put on a small monthly dose of ivermectin instead of moxidectin, which should also kill and shrink the worms slowly over time. If small amounts of doxycycline were also used to kill the Wolbachia, it might be possible that most cats would survive the elimination of the heartworms.

It seems that reducing the inflammatory effects of heartworms and their antigens is the best route to take for small animals. Supportive therapy such as a nutritious diet, clean water and whatever else can be done to improve the cat's or ferret's health is also important for its recovery from a heartworm infection.

LUCY'S STORY

I decided to treat my dog Lucy's heartworm infection myself. This was a decision that slowly emerged on its own while I was doing my initial research. Surprisingly, the adulticide melarsomine became available again before Lucy got infected. However, after learning about its downside I decided that it wasn't for us. I just couldn't put her life at risk at those odds.

When I first discovered that Lucy had a heartworm infection I was afraid that the infection was severe and would kill her. My imagination ran wild, but in reality she only had a moderate infection. Her breathing was labored for a year before the heartworm test but that was the only symptom she had.

I began by mixing my own ivermectin dilution so I could save money while having more control over how much of the drug I gave her. I began by giving her preventative doses of ivermectin once every 30 days and then lowered this dose to once every 45 days once she tested negative on the antigen test. Some sources recommend giving ivermectin once every week to treat heartworm. But once a month will still shrink, make infertile and kill the heartworms eventually.

I also purchased some doxycycline on the internet and verified that the recommended dosage was 10 mg/kg BID for 4 weeks. The bottle had pills that contained 100mg of doxycycline hyclate each. Lucy weighs 70 pounds or 32 kilograms so I crushed up 3 pills and gave her 300 milligrams twice a day.

I became concerned when her overall mood and physical well-being deteriorated during the time I was giving her the doxycycline. She just didn't feel well and would sleep all day. I decided to lower the dose to 300 milligrams once a day and then lowered it again during the fourth week to 100 milligrams once a day.

Doxycycline is very fat soluble so I applied the "less is more" strategy because the drug will build up over time in the body. What is most important is that it has enough time and concentration in the blood to sterilize the female worms and eventually kill them. 4 weeks should be enough time to allow this to happen, and more than this is probably overkill. The worms will slowly die and disintegrate but will still show positive on antigen heartworm tests until they are completely gone which can take many months.

I was sure to give Lucy a couple probiotic supplements everyday while I was dosing her with the doxycycline. Remember, the natural beneficial bacteria get destroyed by the doxycycline so it is very important to replenish it. Probiotics can be found at most stores that carry vitamins and other supplements. Yogurt can also be used to help replenish the animal's natural bacteria.

I was also sure to have fresh clean water available to her at all times. I also began to cook homemade food for both Lucy and Molly using a mixture of 1 cup of meat, 1 cup of grains, 1 cup of a vegetable and a very small amount of salt. Salt will only increase edema (water retention) produced by the heartworms. In addition I gave them a vitamin, fish oil and mineral supplement a few times a week.

"The physical signs of healing from heartworm disease are truly amazing to witness."

I also used aspirin to treat the inflammation inside her arteries while the heartworms were still alive and after they started to decompose. Aspirin works very well in dogs to slow or reverse the narrowing of the arteries caused by the damage and scarring initiated by the heartworms. Aspirin is also the only safe over the counter pain medication for dogs.

After only a couple months Lucy's breathing became much more calm and normal. She sleeps much better and without the need to always catch her breath. In less than a year she looks and acts 4 years younger and now has a sparkle in her eyes. At the end of a year I took her in again to get tested for heartworms and was overjoyed to hear the negative results.

Once the process of healing has begun, an animal will recover their health amazingly fast. This healing can be clearly seen as early as 4 weeks. In the beginning the lesions in the arteries rapidly decrease in size. Within one year all pulmonary arterial surfaces undergo a radical transformation resembling their original state.

Also, within a year of heartworm elimination, the main and lobar pulmonary arteries are reduced in size. The pulmonary arterial pressure returns to baseline levels which takes off the huge extra load that the heart has to carry caused from arterial inflammation. The physical signs of healing from heartworm disease are truly amazing to witness.

Aspirin Therapy

In the 1980's, there were many studies done on the effects of aspirin in dogs with active heartworm infections. It was shown time and time again that even small doses of aspirin given consistently over time could heal the lesions inside the arteries even while the heartworms were still alive and healthy and would protect the arteries from embolism around dead and decaying heartworms.

Aspirin would do this by modifying the way platelets in the blood stick to the lesions which would reverse or halt the narrowing of the inside of the arteries. This would allow the blood to move freely effectively keeping pulmonary pressure down and closer to normal.

The small amount of aspirin needed for these marvelous effects in dogs is low enough to usually not cause the gastric problems that higher doses of aspirin do. After repeated testing it was discovered that 7 mg/kg of aspirin given daily would protect the arteries and begin to heal the existing damage. Even 3 mg/kg of aspirin given once every 6 days has proven to impede progression of arterial disease.

With this information it seems possible to start a dog with even far progressed heartworm disease on a regimen of aspirin and a monthly preventative dose of ivermectin as the sole method to treat both the symptoms and the infection. Or, it could be possible to only give the dog aspirin while improving their overall health through nutrition and other means which would boost their immune system and allow their bodies to heal from heartworms naturally.

Even though both the above examples are valid, most contemporary veterinarians have no idea about aspirin's healing effects on heartworm disease. A few years back, aspirin found favor in the veterinarians office. But more recently, animal medicine has withdrawn its support of aspirin for treating heartworm disease.

This is surprising, because in the 1980's there were many studies showing clear evidence that aspirin brought about resolution of pulmonary hypertension in dogs by reversing the narrowing of the arteries. I contacted the American Heartworm Society and asked them why they are against aspirin even in light of such overwhelming evidence. In response, they cited a study from the University of Queensland in Australia about the effect of a drug called prednisone on the inflammatory reaction of the arteries to worm fragments and antigens.

The study showed how just like aspirin, a low dose of the corticosteroid prednisone at 1 mg/kg body weight given once every other day reduced or reversed the pathology associated with the heartworms. The study referenced the fact that Australia was already using prednisone to alleviate inflammation while most other countries sought the elimination of heartworms as the first priority.

In more recent times, prednisone has been accepted as part of the routine treatment of heartworm disease. In speculation, it seems that aspirin has been shunned and forgotten because it can cause adverse reactions when taken in combination with other anti-inflammatory drugs (NSAIDs) such as prednisone. Also, aspirin is freely available but prednisone is much easier to control.

Prednisone has many more adverse side effects than aspirin does. Also, the body can become dependent on it, which would necessitate slowly reducing the dose versus stopping all at once. However, aspirin has been shown to be safe in dogs when taken in small amounts. In low doses its predominant side effects are gastric upset or stomach ulcerations. It's easy to keep the side effects at a minimum by giving the dog enteric-coated aspirin on a full stomach.

It has also been shown that in combination with the adulticide thiacetarsamide, prednisone might slow down the death of the heartworms and inhibit inflammatory clearance of fragments of dead heartworms. In comparison, aspirin is very effective in reducing pulmonary arterial disease without any effect on the kill rate or the clearance of dead heartworm fragments in dogs.

I gave Lucy 3 mg/kg of aspirin once every 6 days for more than year. Since she weighs 30 kg, a baby aspirin of 81 mg is all she needs. If your dog has worse symptoms then you might consider giving 7 mg/kg of aspirin 5 days out of every 7. On that regimen Lucy would get 210 mg of aspirin or roughly 2 and a half baby aspirins at 80 mg each. An even better regimen might prove to be 4 mg/kg of body weigh given daily.

Cats and ferrets should not be given aspirin and might instead benefit from very low doses of prednisone given every other day instead. Cats don't break down aspirin effectively, and the drug can build up to toxic concentrations. Ferrets are quite delicate creatures and aspirin can prove to be too much to handle for its small body.

THE FUTURE OF HEARTWORM DISEASE

There are many exciting discoveries waiting for mankind in the years ahead. Some of these will be huge advances in the way we treat disease. Heartworm disease will no doubt benefit. These methods could be something that we have yet to even imagine yet.

Two organic compounds that should be of great promise in the years to come for treating and preventing heartworm disease are stabilized allicin derived from garlic and black seed oil from the Nigella Sativa plant. These great substances given to us by nature could unlock the answer to curing heartworm disease.

Human beings have been healing a wide spectrum of diseases in animals and themselves with garlic since the beginning. This ancient food crop has been cultivated and harvested for thousands of years. Garlic is also the earliest known plants to be used for treatment of disease and maintenance of health.

The evidence for garlic's long history with mankind can be found in ancient texts all over the world. Each culture came to understand garlic's potential on their own and completely separated from each other. It has also been used for the healing of animals in the care of human beings for just as long. This includes canines and felines as well as many other living beings.

Modern science is only now catching up with garlic's rich history as a miracle healer. It is a natural anti-parasite and helps rid the body of worms, fleas, ticks and heartworms. There is evidence that garlic destroys the protective coating on the heartworm's skin. It also builds the immune system, aiding and enabling the body to heal itself from all manner of disease.

Despite the incredible amount of time that has proven the benefits of garlic in our pets, there is a fad of misinformation about garlic that has been propagated online. People are spreading the false message that garlic can cause a condition called Heinz factor anemia in dogs and cats. Heinz factor anemia is essentially the death of some red blood cells which causes the anemia to form.

The culprit that causes Heinz factor anemia is actually a compound called n-propyl disulfide. It can be found in copious amounts in onions, shallots, chives and leeks and other species in the genus Allium. It can also be found in garlic but in much smaller amounts. Because of this it is safe to feed your pets reasonable amounts of garlic without any harmful effects. The keyword here is "reasonable", just use your better judgement.

The best way to take it internally is to chop and mince fresh and organic garlic and let it sit for about 15 minutes before eating it raw. By letting it sit you are allowing a compound in the fresh garlic to form called allicin which is a potent antibiotic. Afterwards, you can simply mix it in your animal's food.

By feeding your pets some fresh garlic everyday you are helping their bodies resist disease of all sorts, including the ill effects of a heartworm infection. The garlic will help repel mosquitoes and other parasites, further aiding the animal's health. Be careful with garlic when also giving aspirin as both are blood thinners.

The compound called allicin that is formed when the garlic is cut or crushed has even more potential for treating heartworm disease. But until recently, allicin has been an extremely unstable compound which has made it virtually impossible to produce commercially.

However, a patent to create a stabilized form of allicin was recently submitted and already there are products that contain it. Look for "stabilized allicin", not products that claim to produce allicin inside the body.

The discovery of using stabilized allicin to treat heartworm infections is monumental. First of all, researchers have found that allicin is more effective than the tetracycline antibiotics such as doxycycline. Remember that doxycycline is now used to kill the Wolbachia bacteria that live inside the heartworm which effectively sterilizes, initiates its death and lowers the damage done when the heartworm dies. Imagine the potential of a natural antibiotic to do the same job as doxycycline but without the toxic side effects.

Allicin might prove to be the missing compound in treating dogs, cats and ferrets for a heartworm infection. By first sterilizing the heartworm it will eliminate new microfilariae from entering the blood stream. Also, the death of the Wolbachia will trigger the death of the heartworms. And when they die, the detrimental effects of their passing inside the arteries will be drastically reduced. This is especially important in cats and ferrets, since the death of a single heartworm can lead to their demise.

Stabilized allicin has many of the benefits of whole garlic but can be gentler. There is little smell since allicin becomes absorbed in the gut before it breaks down. Stabilized allicin also effectively repels fleas, ticks and mosquitoes.

There are many products that contain stabilized allicin in the market today. However, the liquid containing stabilized allicin might be the most cost effective and easiest to administer. Just add the liquid to their food, your pet probably won't even notice it.

Garlic and allicin are wonderful gifts of the earth and we can all do well to use this more in our lives. Look for stabilized allicin to take the medical world by storm, as it is the only antibiotic that the resistant strains of bacteria are effected by.

THE BLESSED BLACK SEED

Black seed is potent medicine that has been used since the beginning of recorded history. Also known as black cumin or by its botanical name Nigella sativa, black seed has been used daily in the middle east for every sickness.

Incredibly, black seed has only begun to become known in the western world as its healing abilities are told from person to person. Cultivated in Egypt, Pakistan, Turkey, Iran and Iraq the black seed needs a dry and hot climate to thrive in sandy soil. The plant has beautiful blue flowers and ornamental seed pods.

Black seed and its oil has the ability to stabilize and strengthen the body's immune system. A healthy immune system reacts to attacks from the outside world while eliminating harmful intruders that manage to get inside. A healthy immune system can rescue the body from a heartworm infection on its own.

Black seed is a powerful anthelmintic which means it expels parasites. It is also a potent anti-inflammatory and anti-spasmodic which will reduce the hypertension that is produced by a heartworm infection. It's also a pain killer and protects the body from liver damage and radiation while balancing the body's glucose levels.

There have been hundreds of university studies on this amazing herb since it was discovered by the western world, most within the past decade. And its anti-tumor and anti-cancer effects are becoming infamous.

Black seed oil contains the most potent form of the medicine contained in the plant and is the easiest to take. A small amount goes a long way, but since the seeds have been shown to be virtually toxic free, the seeds and oil can be given generously to most living creatures.

For now, black seed oil can be obtained online in the western world. But I expect it to be carried in stores once its healing abilities become more publicized. Some companies are already using the black seed in their natural heartworm medicines so it is surely catching on.

Black seed is an amazing herb that heals the body in many ways. Its effects almost need to be seen and felt to be believed. Watch for this potent herb to take center stage in the healing medicines of the world. Truly, black seed can be given to your pets without fear of toxic effects and with the knowledge that it will aid their body in eliminating all parasites including heartworms.

"Simply starting your dog on a monthly dose of ivermectin is a valid treatment option."

I hope that the research that was done for this book will spark further research in the life giving attributes of garlic and black seed for our pet's health. There will no doubt be other plants and compounds that have yet to be discovered that will also aid our animals in ridding themselves of heartworms.

All the major pharmaceuticals used in the treatment of heartworm were perfected by using inhumane methods of testing on animals. There are less cruel ways of finding valuable data on the efficacy of drugs and natural remedies. And I hope that the insights gleamed from this book that might fuel future research, will not be at the expense of an animal's life.

THINGS TO CONSIDER

If you have a pet with a heartworm infection or live in an area that is endemic for the parasite you will have many things to consider. By now you know more about heartworms than most of the population and you can use that knowledge to help guide you along the ocean of choices that awaits you.

Those choices might be influenced by your budget, fear, doubt and an infinite combination of factors. What we can both agree upon is improving the health of your pets. Although the choices are not always clear, you can imagine the outcome you want to happen for your pet and keep that image clear in your mind. Prayer might be helpful during these times as well.

Sometimes the decision might be to not treat your pet with conventional veterinarian medicine. It is true that there are toxic and expensive drugs involved in that process. We want the healing of our pet's bodies without weakening their immune and other bodily systems. Just because we hear that time is of the essence, we now know that even the slow elimination of heartworms will sometimes be the most beneficial.

Alternatively, you might decide to use a treatment of your own design out of what you learned already. Just make sure to test your pet every year and if they become positive again raise the bar of treatment until they test negative again.

Simply starting your dog on a monthly dose of ivermectin is a valid treatment option. At least the infection will be neutralized and the elimination of the heartworms will be well on its way.

Regardless of what you decide it is always helpful to improve the overall health of your dog, cat or ferret. Clean fresh water, good nutrition with fresh foods, vitamin and mineral supplements, probiotics, plenty of fresh air and exercise and a positive loving environment are all things you can improve upon now and are great ways of sharing your love with your animals.

I wish you and your pets the greatest of health and happiness. I am confident that this book will guide you in making the right decisions for them. Relax, take a deep breath and trust.

CHAPTER ONE

Al-Khalili, J. (2011). *Black holes wormholes and time machines.* Taylor & Francis Group.

Dolgin, E. (2010). Animal testing alternatives come alive in US. *Johns Hopkins Bloomberg School of Public Health.* Retrieved from altweb.jhsph.edu/news/2010/nature1210.html

Dowling, P. (2006). Pharmacogenetics: It's not just about Ivermectin in collies. *Can Vet J, 47*(12), 1165-1168.

Heartworm treatment supply runs dry. (2011). *The Daily Tribune News - Heartworm Treatment Supply Runs Dry.* Retrieved from daily-tribune.com/view/full_story/15166604/article-Heartworm-treatment-supply-runs-dry

Putney, M. (2008). Being a mouse on death row: Researchers look for alternatives to animal testing. *Science & Spirit, 19*(1), 46-47. doi: 10.3200/SSPT.19.1.46-47

Shortage of Immiticide for heartworm treatment. (2011, October). *DogAware.com News Archive:.* Retrieved from dogaware.com/articles/newsimmiticide.html

CHAPTER TWO

Asimacopoulos, P., Katras, A., & Christie, B. (1992). Pulmonary dirofilariasis: The largest single-hospital experience. *Chest, 102*(3), 851-855. doi: 10.1378/chest.102.3.851

Bedin, M., Petterino, C., Gallo, E., Selleri, P., & Morgante, M. (2007). Clinical pathological findings in an owl (Athene noctua) with microfilaraemia in Italy. *Journal of Veterinary Medicine Series A, 54*(3), 128-130. doi: 10.1111/j.1439-0442.2007.00905.x

Billups, J., Schenken, J., & Beaver, P. (1980). Subcutaneous dirofilariasis in Nebraska. *Arch Pathol Lab Med., 104*(1), 11-13.

Brown, C. (2006, April 12). Coyote carcasses yield info about coyote diet and health. *Coyote Bytes - Official Newspaper of The Narragansett Bay Coyote Study.* Retrieved from theconservationagency.org/coyotes/coyote_bytes/coyote_bytes_2006apr12.htm

Carroll, E., Faust, E., Thomas, P., & Jones, J. (1941). Discovery of human heartworm infection in New Orleans. *The Journal of Parasitology, 27*(2), 115-116.

Christensen, B., & Shelton, M. (1978). Laboratory observations on the insusceptibility of raccoons to Dirofilaria immitis. *J Wildl Dis, 14*(1), 22-23.

Ciferri, F. (1981). Human pulmonary dirofilariasis in the west. *Western Journal of Medicine, 134*(2), 158-162.

Dirofilaria immitis. (2011, March 12). *YouTube.* Retrieved from youtube.com/watch?v=ZBdLnAkFjJA

Dissanaike, A., Ramalingam, S., Fong, A., Pathmayokan, S., Thomas, V., & Kan, S. (1977). Filaria in the vitreous of the eye of man in Peninsular Malaysia. *Am J Trop Med Hyg., 26*(1), 1143-1147.

Faust, E., Thomas, E., & Jones, J. (1941). Discovery of human heartworm infection in New Orleans. *The Journal of Parasitology, 27,* 115-122.

Feldman, R., & Holden, M. (1974). Meningeal irritation, hemoptysis and eosinophili - A case of human dirofilariasis. *JAMA, 228,* 1018-1019.

Fulton, A. (1982). The rise of the eucaryotic cell symbiosis in cell evolution. *Cell, 28*(3), 673-674. doi: 10.1016/0092-8674(82)90222-7

Genchi, C., Kramer, L. H., & Rivasi, F. (2011). Dirofilarial infections in Europe. *Vector-Borne and Zoonotic Diseases, 11*(10), 1307-1317. doi: 10.1089/vbz.2010.0247

Grinder, M., & Krausman, P. (2001). Morbidity-mortality factors and survival or an urban coyote population in Arizona. *Journal of Wildlife Diseases*, 312-317.

Gurney, R. (2009). What about parasites? *What about Parasites*. Retrieved from creation.com/what-about-parasites

Gutierrez, T., Crystal, J. D., Zvonok, A. M., Makriyannis, A., & Hohmann, A. G. (2011). Self-medication of a cannabinoid CB2 agonist in an animal model of neuropathic pain. *Pain*, *152*(9), 1976-1987. doi: 10.1016/j.pain.2011.03.038

Hoerauf, A., & Rao, R. U. (2007). *Wolbachia: A bug's life in another bug*. Basel: Karger.

Huffman, M. A., & Hirata, S. (2004). An experimental study of leaf swallowing in captive chimpanzees: Insights into the origin of a self-medicative behavior and the role of social learning. *Primates*, *45*(2), 113-118. doi: 10.1007/s10329-003-0065-5

Huffman, M. A. (2003). Animal self-medication and ethno-medicine: Exploration and exploitation of the medicinal properties of plants. *Proceedings of the Nutrition Society*, *62*(02), 371. doi: 10.1079/PNS2003257

Jernigan, K. A. (2009). Barking up the same tree: A comparison of ethnomedicine and canine ethnoveterinary medicine among the Aguaruna. *Journal of Ethnobiology and Ethnomedicine*, *5*(1), 33. doi: 10.1186/1746-4269-5-33

Kamalakannan, S., Madhiyazhagan, P., Dhandapani, A., Murugan, K., & Barnard, D. (2010). (Euphorbiaceae) leaf extract phytochemicals: Toxicity to the filariasis vector (Diptera: Culicidae). *Vector-Borne and Zoonotic Diseases*, *10*(8), 817-820. doi: 10.1089/vbz.2009.0081

Kaneda, Y., Asami, K., Kawai, T., & Sakuma, M. (1980). A case of human Infection with dirofilaria in the subcutaneous tissue. *Jap J Parasit*, *29*, 245-249.

Kawabata, A., Nakagaki, K., Yoshida, M., & Shirota, K. (2008). Histopathological comparison of pulmonary artery lesions between raccoon dogs (Nyctereutes procyonoides) and domestic dogs experimentally Infected with Dirofilaria immitis. *Journal of Veterinary Medical Science*, *70*(3), 301-303. doi: 10.1292/jvms.70.301

Levin, B. R., & Rozen, D. E. (2006). Non-inherited antibiotic resistance. *Nature Reviews Microbiology*, *4*(7), 556-562. doi: 10.1038/nrmicro1445

Mazzariol, S., Cassini, R., Voltan, L., Aresu, L., & Frangipane di Regalbono, A. (2010). Heartworm (Dirofilaria immitis) infection in a leopard (Panthera pardus pardus) housed in a zoological park in north-eastern Italy. *Parasites & Vectors*, *3*(1), 25. doi: 10.1186/1756-3305-3-25

Merkel, J., Jones, H. I., Whiteman, N. K., Gottdenker, N., Vargas, H., Travis, E. K., ... Parker, P. G. (2007). Microfilariae In Galápagos penguins (Spheniscus mendiculus) And flightless cormorants (Phalacrocorax Harrisi): Genetics, morphology, and prevalence. *Journal of Parasitology*, *93*(3), 495-503. doi: 10.1645/GE-1009R.1

Merriam-Webster's collegiate dictionary. (2003). Springfield, MA: Merriam-Webster.

Moorhouse, D. (1978). Dirofilaria immiis: A cause of human intra-ocular infection. *Infection*, *6*(4), 192-193.

Nakagaki, K., Yoshida, M., Nogami, S., & Nakagaki, K. (2007). Experimental infection of Dirofilaria immitis in raccoon dogs. *Journal of Parasitology*, *93*(2), 432-434. doi: 10.1645/GE-1042R.1

Nishimura, T., Kondo, K., & Shoho, C. (1964). Human infection with a subcutaneous Dirofilaria immitis. *Biken Journal*, *7*, 1-8.

Orihel, T. C., & Eberhard, M. L. (1998). Zoontic filariasis. *Clin Microbiol Rev., 11*(2), 366-381.

Pappas, L., & Lunzman, A. (1985). Canine heartworm in the domestic and wild canids of southeastern Nebraska. *The Journal of Parasitology, 71*(6).

Raman, R., & Kandula, S. (2008). Zoopharmacognosy. *Resonance, 13*(3), 245-253. doi: 10.1007/s12045-008-0038-5

Robles, M., Aregullin, M., West, J., & Rodriguez, E. (1995). Recent studies on the zoopharmacognosy, pharmacology and neurotoxicology of sesquiterpene lactones. *Planta Medica, 61*(03), 199-203. doi: 10.1055/s-2006-958055

Roy, B., Chirurgi, V., & Theis, J. (1993). Pulmonary dirofilariasis in California. *Western Journal of Medicine, 158*(1), 74-76.

Sacks, B., & Blejwas, K. (2000). Effects of canine heartworm (Dirofilaria immitis) on body condition and activity of free-ranging coyotes (Canis latrans). *Can. J. Zool., 78*, 1042-1051.

Sacks, B. (1998). Increasing prevalence of canine heartworm in coyotes from California. *Journal of Wildlife Diseases*, 386-89.

Siers, S., Merkel, J., Bataille, A., Vargas, F., & Parker, P. (2010). Ecological correlates of microfilariae prevalence in endangered Galapagos birds. *J Parasitol., 96*(2), 259-272.

Simmons, J., Nicholson, W., Hill, E., & Briggs, D. (1980). Occurrence of (Dirofilaria immitis) in gray fox (Urocyon cinereoargenteus) in Alabama and Georgia. *Jwildlifedis, 16*(2), 225-228.

Smith, L., & Schillaci, R. (1986). Pulmonary dirofilariasis in humans-pneumonitis that evolved to a lung nodule. *Western Journal of Medicine, 145*(4), 516-519.

Snyder, D., Hamir, A., Hanlon, C., & Rupprecht, C. (1989). Dirofilaria immitis in a raccoon (Procyon lotor). *J Wildl Dis., 25*(1), 130-131.

Stadler, B., & Dixon, A. F. (2008). *Mutualism: Ants and their insect partners.* Cambridge: Cambridge University Press.

Tada, I., Sakaguchi, Y., & Eto, K. (1979). Dirofilaria in the abdominal cavity of a man in Japan. *Am J Trop Med Hyg., 28*(6), 988-990.

Theis, J., Gilson, A., Simon, G., Bradshaw, B., & Clark, D. (2001). Case report: Unusual location of Dirofilaria immitis in a 28-year-old man necessitates orchiectomy. *American Society of Tropical Medicine, 64*(5-6), 317-322.

Thomas, B. (2009, February 2). Parasitic worms evolved the wrong direction. *Parasitic Worms Evolved the Wrong Direction.* Retrieved from icr.org/article/parasitic-worms-evolved-wrong-direction/

Thomas, B. (2010, December). Parasitic worms help heal intestines. *Parasitic Worms Help Heal Intestines.* Retrieved from icr.org/article/5845/

Thurman, J., Johnson, B., & Lichtenfels, J. (1984). Dirofilariasis with arteriosclerosis in a horse. *J Am Vet Med Assoc., 185*(5), 532-533.

Traversa, D., Di Cesare, A., & Conboy, G. (2010). Canine and feline cardiopulmonary parasitic nematodes in Europe: Emerging and underestimated. *Parasites & Vectors, 3*(1), 62. doi: 10.1186/1756-3305-3-62

Villalba, J. J., & Provenza, F. D. (2007). Self-medication and homeostatic behaviour in herbivores: Learning about the benefits of nature's pharmacy. *Animal, 1*(09). doi: 10.1017/S1751731107000134

CHAPTER THREE

Amoils, S. (2005). Horizontal gene transfer: Analysing incompatibility — Wolbachia on the couch. *Nature Reviews Microbiology, 3*(9), 667-667. doi: 10.1038/nrmicro1242

Aranda, C., Panyella, O., Eritja, R., & Castellà, J. (1998). Canine filariasis. Importance and transmission in the Baix Llobregat area, Barcelona (Spain). *Vet Parasitol.*, *77*(4), 267-275.

Baldo, L., Prendini, L., Corthals, A., & Werren, J. (2007). Wolbachia are present in southern African scorpions and cluster with supergroup F. *Curr Microbiol*, *55*(5), 367-373.

Berticat, C., Rousset, F., Raymond, M., Berthomieu, A., & Weill, M. (2002). High Wolbachia density in insecticide-resistant mosquitoes. *Proceedings of the Royal Society B: Biological Sciences*, *269*(1498), 1413-1416. doi: 10.1098/rspb.2002.2022

Brattig, N., Racz, P., Hoerauf, A., & Büttner, D. (2011). Strong expression of TGF-beta in human host tissues around subcutaneous Dirofilaria repens. *Parasitol Res*, *108*(6), 1347-1354.

Calow, P. (1992). Book Review: Invertebrates. Richard C. Brusca, Gary J. Brusca. *The Quarterly Review of Biology*, *67*(2), 215.

Cancrini, G., Allende, E., Favia, G., Bornay, F., Antón, F., & Simón, F. (2000). Canine dirofilariosis in two cities of southeastern Spain. *Veterinary Parasitology*, *92*(1), 81-86. doi: 10.1016/S0304-4017(00)00270-3

Church, E., Georgi, J., & Robson, D. (1976). Analysis of the microfilarial periodicity of Dirofilaria immitis. *Cornell Vet.*, *66*(3), 333-346.

Fenn, K., Conlon, C., Jones, M., Quail, M. A., Holroyd, N. E., Parkhill, J., & Blaxter, M. (2006). Phylogenetic relationships of the Wolbachia of nematodes and arthropods. *PLoS Pathogens*, *2*(10), E94. doi: 10.1371/journal.ppat.0020094

Foster, J., Ganatra, M., Kamal, I., Ware, J., Makarova, K., Ivanova, N., ... Slatko, B. (2005). The Wolbachia genome of Brugia malayi: Endosymbiont evolution within a human pathogenic nematode. *PLoS Biology*, *3*(4), E121. doi: 10.1371/journal.pbio.0030121

Furtado, A. P., Melo, F. V., Giese, E. G., & Dos Santos, J. N. (2010). Morphological redescription of Dirofilaria immitis. *Journal of Parasitology*, *96*(3), 499-504. doi: 10.1645/GE-2178.1

Geary, J., Satti, M., Moreno, Y., Madrill, N., Whitten, D., Headley, S., ... Mackenzie, C. (2012). First analysis of the secretome of the canine heartworm, Dirofilaria immitis. *Parasit Vectors*, *10*, 1186-1756.

Gould, F., Magori, K., & Huang, Y. (2006). Genetic strategies for controlling mosquito-borne diseases. *American Scientist*, *94*(3), 238.

Grandi, G., Morchon, R., Kramer, L., Kartashev, V., & Simon, F. (2008). Wolbachia in Dirofilaria repens, an agent causing human subcutaneous dirofilariasis. *Journal of Parasitology*, *94*(6), 1421-1423. doi: 10.1645/GE-1575.1

Hertig, M., & Wolbach, S. (1924). Studies on rickettsia-like micro-organisms in insects. *J Med Res*, *44*(3), 329-374.

Hoerauf, A., & Rao, R. U. (2007). *Wolbachia: A bug's life in another bug*. Basel: Karger.

Hyman, L. H. (1963). Book Review: Invertebrate Zoology. Robert D. Barnes. *The Quarterly Review of Biology*, *38*(4), 399.

Kaiser, W., Huguet, E., Casas, J., Commin, C., & Giron, D. (2010). Plant green-island phenotype induced by leaf-miners is mediated by bacterial symbionts. *Proceedings of the Royal Society B: Biological Sciences*, *277*(1692), 2311-2319. doi: 10.1098/rspb.2010.0214

Liu, H., Fu, Y., Jiang, D., Li, G., Xie, J., Cheng, J., ... Yi, X. (2010). Widespread Horizontal Widespread horizontal gene transfer from double-stranded RNA viruses to eukaryotic nuclear genomesTransfer from Double-Stranded RNA Viruses to

Eukaryotic Nuclear Genomes. *Journal of Virology, 84*(22), 11876-11887. doi: 10.1128/JVI.00955-10

Longstaffe, J. (1984). Helminths, arthropods and protozoa of domesticated animals (7th edition). *Transactions of the Royal Society of Tropical Medicine and Hygiene, 78*(3), 329.

Muro, A., Genchi, C., Cordero, M., & Simón, F. (1999). Human dirofilariasis in the European Union. *Parasitol Today, 15*(9), 386-389.

Nogami, S., Murasugi, E., Shimazaki, K., Maeda, R., Harasawa, R., & Nakagaki, K. (2000). Quantitative analysis of microfilarial periodicity of Dirofilaria immitis in cats. *Veterinary Parasitology, 92*(3), 227-232.

Poinar, G. (2011). The evolutionary history of nematodes. *Over Three Centuries of Scholarly Publishing.* Retrieved April 03, 2013, from brill.com/evolutionary-history-nematodes

Rawlings, C. A. (1986). *Heartworm disease in dogs and cats.* Philadelphia: Saunders.

Simón, F., Morchón, R., Rodríguez-Barbero, A., López-Belmonte, J., Grandi, G., & Genchi, C. (2008). Dirofilaria immitis and Wolbachia-derived antigens: Its effect on endothelial mammal cells. *Veterinary Parasitology, 158*(3), 223-231. doi: 10.1016/j.vetpar.2008.09.010

Simon, F., & Genchi, C. (2001). *Heartworm infection in humans and animals.* Salamanca: Universidad de Salamanca.

Sloss, M. W., & Kemp, R. L. (1978). *Veterinary clinical parasitology.* Ames: Iowa State University Press.

Talukder, M., Ueda, K., Hajime, T., Kanako, S., Kawamura, S., & Hikasa, Y. (2008). Evaluation of protective immunity against experimental Dirofilaria immitis infection in beagle dogs. *Bangladesh Journal of Veterinary Medicine, 5*(1). doi: 10.3329/bjvm.v5i1.1323

Teixeira, L., Ferreira, Á, & Ashburner, M. (2008). The bacterial symbiont Wolbachia induces resistance to RNA viral infections in Drosophila melanogaster (L. Keller, Ed.). *PLoS Biology, 6*(12), E2. doi: 10.1371/journal.pbio.1000002

Werren, J. H., Windsor, D., & Guo, L. (1995). Distribution of Wolbachia among neotropical arthropods. *Proceedings of the Royal Society B: Biological Sciences, 262*(1364), 197-204. doi: 10.1098/rspb.1995.0196

Yong, E. (2011, August 11). Defeating dendue by releasing mosquitoes with virus-blocking bacteria. *Not Exactly Rocket Science.* Retrieved from blogs.discovermagazine.com/notrocketscience/2011/08/24/defeating-dengue-by-releasing-mosquitoes-with-virus-blocking-bacteria/

Young, E. (2012, December 22). *Genetically-modified mosquitoes fight malaria by outcompeting normal ones.* Retrieved April 03, 2013, from scienceblogs.com/notrocketscience/2008/10/21/geneticallymodified-mosquitoes-fight-malaria-by-outcompeting/

CHAPTER FOUR

Abboti, P. K. (1961). Dirofilaria immitis In the peritoneal cavity. *Australian Veterinary Journal, 37*(12), 467-467. doi: 10.1111/j.1751-0813.1961.tb08712.x

Atkinson, K., Fine, D., Thombs, L., Gorelick, J., & Durham, H. (2009). Evaluation of pimobendan and n-terminal probrain natriuretic peptide in the treatment of pulmonary hypertension secondary to degenerative mitral valve disease in dogs. *Journal of Veterinary Internal Medicine.* doi: 10.1111/j.1939-1676.2009.0390.x

Atwell, R. (1992). Dirofilaria immitis in cats. *Australian Veterinary Journal, 69*(2),

44-44. doi: 10.1111/j.1751-0813.1992.tb07440.x

Balak, N. (2008). Unilateral partial hemilaminectomy in the removal of a large spinal ependymoma. *The Spine Journal, 8*(6), 1030-1036. doi: 10.1016/j.spinee.2007.07.001

Bateman, S. W., Mathews, K. A., & Abrams-Ogg, A. C. (1998). Disseminated intravascular coagulation in dogs: Review of the literature. *Journal of Veterinary Emergency and Critical Care, 8*(1), 29-45. doi: 10.1111/j.1476-4431.1998.tb00132.x

Boswood, A., Dukes-McEwan, J., French, A., Little, C., Patteson, M., Swift, S., ... Willis, R. (2008). Treatment of congestive heart failure in dogs. *Veterinary Record, 163*(17), 520-520. doi: 10.1136/vr.163.17.520

Cho, W., & Trow, T. K. (2007). Combination therapy in the treatment of pulmonary arterial hypertension: Can that dog hunt? *Clinical Pulmonary Medicine, 14*(4), 242-243. doi: 10.1097/CPM.0b013e3180cac712

Chunn, C. F., & Harkins, H. N. (1941). Alimentary Azotemia. *The American Journal of the Medical Sciences, 201*(5), 745-748. doi: 10.1097/00000441-194105000-00016

Cottrell, K. (2004, October 1). Heartworm Disease. *Heartworm Disease.* Retrieved from miamiferret.org/heartworm.htm

Davidson, B. L., Rozanski, E. A., Tidwell, A. S., & Hoffman, A. M. (2006). Pulmonary thromboembolism in a heartworm-positive cat. *Journal of Veterinary Internal Medicine, 20*(4), 1037. doi: 10.1892/0891-6640(2006)20[1037:PTIAHC]2.0.CO;2

Davis, J. O., Pechet, M. M., Ball, W. C., Goodkind, M. J., & Casper, A. (1957). Increased aldosterone secretion in dogs with right-sided congestive heart failure and in dogs with thoracic inferior vena cava constriction. *Journal of Clinical Investigation, 36*(5), 689-694. doi: 10.1172/JCI103470

Dingman, P., Levy, J. K., Kramer, L. H., Johnson, C. M., Lappin, M. R., Greiner, E. C., ... Morchon, R. (2010). Association of Wolbachia with heartworm disease in cats and dogs. *Veterinary Parasitology, 170*(1-2), 50-60. doi: 10.1016/j.vetpar.2010.01.037

Estrin, M. A., Wehausen, C. E., Jessen, C. R., & Lee, J. A. (2006). Disseminated intravascular coagulation in cats. *Journal of Veterinary Internal Medicine, 20*(6), 1334. doi: 10.1892/0891-6640(2006)20[1334:DICIC]2.0.CO;2

Farabaugh, A. E., Freeman, L. M., Rush, J. E., & George, K. L. (2004). Lymphocyte subpopulations and hematologic variables in dogs with congestive heart failure. *Journal of Veterinary Internal Medicine, 18*(4), 505. doi: 10.1892/0891-6640(2004)182.0.CO;2

Fedullo, P., Auger, W., Kerr, K., & Rubin, L. (2002). Chronic thromboembolic pulmonary hypertension. *New England Journal of Medicine, 346*(11), 866-866. doi: 10.1056/NEJM200203143461119

Freeman, L. M., Rush, J. E., Milbury, P. E., & Blumberg, J. B. (2005). Antioxidant status and biomarkers of oxidative stress in dogs with congestive heart failure. *Journal of Veterinary Internal Medicine, 19*(4), 537. doi: 10.1892/0891-6640(2005)19[537:ASABOO]2.0.CO;2

Genchi, C., Rinaldi, L., & Cringoli, G. (2007). *Dirofilaria immitis and D. repens in dog and cat and human infections.* Naples: Veterinary Parasitology and Parasitic Diseases, Dept. of Pathology and Animal Health, Faculty of Veterinary Medicine,University of Naples Federico II.

Genchi, C., Venco, L., Ferrari, N., Mortarino, M., & Genchi, M. (2008). Feline heartworm

(Dirofilaria immitis) infection: A statistical elaboration of the duration of the infection and life expectancy in asymptomatic cats. *Veterinary Parasitology, 158*(3), 177-182. doi: 10.1016/j.vetpar.2008.09.005

Goodwin, J. (1998). The serologic diagnosis of heartworm infection in dogs and cats. *Clinical Techniques in Small Animal Practice, 13*(2), 83-87. doi: 10.1016/S1096-2867(98)80011-X

Grandi, G., Quintavalla, C., Mavropoulou, A., Genchi, M., Gnudi, G., Bertoni, G., & Kramer, L. (2010). A combination of doxycycline and ivermectin is adulticidal in dogs with naturally acquired heartworm disease (Dirofilaria immitis). *Veterinary Parasitology, 169*(3-4), 347-351. doi: 10.1016/j.vetpar.2010.01.025

Grandi, G., Quintavalla, C., Mavropoulou, A., Genchi, M., Gnudi, G., Bertoni, G., & Kramer, L. (2011). Corrigendum to "A combination of doxycycline and ivermectin is adulticidal in dogs with naturally acquired heartworm disease (Dirofilaria immitis)" [Vet. Parasitol. 169 (2010) 347–351]. *Veterinary Parasitology, 177*(1-2), 196. doi: 10.1016/j.vetpar.2010.12.001

Greer, R., Lichtenberger, M., & Kirby, R. (2004). Use of sodium nitroprusside (snp) for treatment of fulminant congestive heart failure (chf) in dogs with mitral regurgitation. *Journal of Veterinary Emergency and Critical Care, 14*(S1), S1-S17. doi: 10.1111/j.1476-4431.2004.t01-28-04035.x

Guyonnet, J., Elliott, J., & Kaltsatos, V. (2009). A preclinical pharmacokinetic and pharmacodynamic approach to determine a dose of spironolactone for treatment of congestive heart failure in dog. *Journal of Veterinary Pharmacology and Therapeutics.* doi: 10.1111/j.1365-2885.2009.01130.x

Hagiwara, M. K., Kogika, M. M., & Malucelli, B. E. (1990). Disseminated intravascular coagulation in dogs with aflatoxicosis. *Journal of Small Animal Practice, 31*(5), 239-243. doi: 10.1111/j.1748-5827.1990.tb00793.x

Heinemann, H. O., Maack, T. M., & Sherman, R. L. (1974). Proteinuria. *The American Journal of Medicine, 56*(1), 71-82. doi: 10.1016/0002-9343(74)90752-9

Hirano, Y., Kitagawa, H., & Sasaki, Y. (1992). Relationship between pulmonary arterial pressure and pulmonary thromboembolism associated with dead worms in canine heartworm disease. *The Journal of Veterinary Medical Science, 54*(5), 897-904. doi: 10.1292/jvms.54.897

Hogle, W. P., & Gobel, B. H. (2003). Disseminated intravascular coagulation. *Clinical Journal of Oncology Nursing, 7*(3), 339-340. doi: 10.1188/03.CJON.339-340

Holt, D. E., Cole, S. G., Anderson, R. B., Miscelis, R. R., & Bridges, C. R. (2005). The canine right caudal and accessory lobe pulmonary veins: Revised anatomical description, clinical relevance, and embryological implications. *Anatomia, Histologia, Embryologia: Journal of Veterinary Medicine Series C, 34*(4), 273-275. doi: 10.1111/j.1439-0264.2005.00610.x

Iizuka, T., Hoshi, K., Ishida, Y., & Sakata, I. (2009). Right atriotomy using total venous inflow occlusion for removal of heartworms in a cat. *Journal of Veterinary Medical Science, 71*(4), 489-491. doi: 10.1292/jvms.71.489

Ishihara, K., Sasaki, Y., & Kitagawa, H. (1986). Development of a flexible alligator forceps : A new instrument for removal of heartworms in the pulmonary arteries of dogs. *The Japanese Journal of Veterinary Science, 48*(5), 989-991. doi: 10.1292/jvms1939.48.989

Ishihara, K., Sasaki, Y., Kitagawa, H., & Hayama, M. (1988). Clinical effects after heartworm removal from pulmonary arteries using flexible alligator forceps in dogs with common dirofilariasis. *The Japanese Journal of Veterinary Science, 50*(3), 723-730. doi: 10.1292/jvms1939.50.723

Jones, D. E., Denny, H. R., & Mullowney, P. C. (1976). Disseminated intravascular coagulation in the dog. *Journal of Small Animal Practice, 17*(6), 387-390. doi: 10.1111/j.1748-5827.1976.tb06975.x

Jones, D. E., Gruffydd-Jones, T. J., & McCULLAGH, K. G. (1980). Disseminated intravascular coagulation in a dog with thoracic neoplasia. *Journal of Small Animal Practice, 21*(5), 303-309. doi: 10.1111/j.1748-5827.1980.tb01251.x

Kaiser, L. (1998). Dirofilaria immitis: Heartworm infection converts histamine-induced constriction to endothelium-dependent relaxation in canine pulmonary artery. *Experimental Parasitology, 88*(2), 146-153. doi: 10.1006/expr.1998.4219

Kelly, J. D. (1974). Canine heartworm disease. *Australian Veterinary Journal, 50*(1), 28-28. doi: 10.1111/j.1751-0813.1974.tb09368.x

Kitagawa, H., Sasaki, Y., Ishihara, K., & Hirano, Y. (1990). Contribution of live heartworms harboring in pulmonary arteries to pulmonary hypertension in dogs with dirofilariasis. *The Japanese Journal of Veterinary Science, 52*(6), 1211-1217. doi: 10.1292/jvms1939.52.1211

Kitagawa, H., Sasaki, Y., Ishihara, K., & Kawakami, M. (1990). Heartworm migration toward right atrium following artificial pulmonary arterial emobolism or injection of heartworm body fluid. *The Japanese Journal of Veterinary Science, 52*(3), 591-599. doi: 10.1292/jvms1939.52.591

Kitagawa, H., Sasaki, Y., Sukigara, T., & Ishihara, K. (1987). Clinical studies on canine dirofilarial hemoglobinuria: Changes in right heart hemodynamics inducing heartworm migration from pulmonary artery. *The Japanese Journal of Veterinary Science, 49*(3), 485-489. doi: 10.1292/jvms1939.49.485

Lai, L., Suematsu, M., Elam, H., & Liang, C. (1996). Differential changes of myocardial - adrenoceptor subtypes and G-proteins in dogs with right-sided congestive heart failure. *European Journal of Pharmacology, 309*(2), 201-208. doi: 10.1016/0014-2999(96)00340-8

Laim, A., Jaggy, A., Forterre, F., Doherr, M. G., Aeschbacher, G., & Glardon, O. (2009). Effects of adjunct electroacupuncture on severity of postoperative pain in dogs undergoing hemilaminectomy because of acute thoracolumbar intervertebral disk disease. *Journal of the American Veterinary Medical Association, 234*(9), 1141-1146. doi: 10.2460/javma.234.9.1141

Levi, M. (2007). Disseminated intravascular coagulation. *Critical Care Medicine, 35*(9), 2191-2195. doi: 10.1097/01.CCM.0000281468.94108.4B

Lewis, B. M., & Dexter, L. (1952). Effects of acute hypoxia on the circulation of the dog. *The American Journal of Medicine, 12*(1), 109-109. doi: 10.1016/0002-9343(52)90179-4

Litster, A., & Atwell, R. (2008). Feline heartworm disease: A clinical review. *Journal of Feline Medicine & Surgery, 10*(2), 137-144. doi: 10.1016/j.jfms.2007.09.007

Litster, A., Atkins, C., & Atwell, R. (2008). Acute death in heartworm-infected cats: Unraveling the puzzle. *Veterinary Parasitology, 158*(3), 196-203. doi: 10.1016/j.vetpar.2008.09.007

MacDonald, K. A., Kittleson, M. D., Munro, C., & Kass, P. (2003). Brain natriuretic peptide concentration in dogs with heart disease and congestive heart failure. *Journal of Veterinary Internal Medicine, 17*(2), 172. doi: 10.1892/0891-6640(2003)0172.3.CO;2

Maia, F. C., McCall, J. W., Jr, V. S., Peixoto, C. A., Supakorndej, P., Supakorndej, N., & Alves, L. C. (2011). Structural and ultrastructural changes in the lungs of cats Felis catus (Linnaeus, 1758) experimentally infected with D. immitis (Leidy, 1856). *Veterinary Parasitology, 176*(4), 304-312. doi: 10.1016/j.vetpar.2011.01.014

Mansfield, C. S., Callanan, J. J., & McAllister, H. (2000). Intra-atrial rhabdomyoma causing chylopericardium and right-sided congestive heart failure in a dog. *Veterinary Record, 147*(10), 264-277. doi: 10.1136/vr.147.10.264

Martinez-Alcaine, M., Ynaraja, E., Corbera, J., & Montoya, J. (2001). Effect of short-term treatment with bumetanide, quinapril and low-sodium diet on dogs with moderate congestive heart failure. *Australian Veterinary Journal, 79*(2), 102-105. doi: 10.1111/j.1751-0813.2001.tb10709.x

Maruyama, H., Miura, T., Sakai, M., Koie, H., Yamaya, Y., Shibuya, H., ... Hasegawa, A. (2004). The incidence of disseminated intravascular coagulation in dogs with malignant tumor. *Journal of Veterinary Medical Science, 66*(5), 573-575. doi: 10.1292/jvms.66.573

Mass, H., Ali, I., Velez, W., & Santiago, O. (1992). Hemodynamics of heartworm infection. *Annals of the New York Academy of Sciences, 653*(1 Tropical Vete), 206-210. doi: 10.1111/j.1749-6632.1992.tb19648.x

McCall, J., Guerrero, J., Genchi, C., & Kramer, L. (2004). Recent advances in heartworm disease. *Veterinary Parasitology, 125*(1-2), 105-130. doi: 10.1016/j.vetpar.2004.05.008

Miller, M. (1998). Canine heartworm disease. *Clinical Techniques in Small Animal Practice, 13*(2), 113-118. doi: 10.1016/S1096-2867(98)80016-9

Mischke, R. (2010). Disseminated intravascular coagulation in dogs: Are scoring systems of value? *The Veterinary Journal, 185*(3), 243-244. doi: 10.1016/j.tvjl.2009.12.009

Molnár, V., Pazár, P., Rigó, D., Máthé, D., Fok, É, Glávits, R., ... Sós, E. (2010). Autochthonous Dirofilaria immitis infection in a ferret with aberrant larval migration in Europe. *Journal of Small Animal Practice, 51*(7), 393-396. doi: 10.1111/j.1748-5827.2010.00950.x

Murray, E. (1995). Physiotherapy for respiratory and cardiac problems. *Physiotherapy, 81*(5), 298-298. doi: 10.1016/S0031-9406(05)66838-1

Nunez, P., & Srinivasan, R. (2007). Electroencephalogram. *Scholarpedia, 2*(2), 1348. doi: 10.4249/scholarpedia.1348

O'Rourke, M., & Hashimoto, J. (2006). The arterial system; its influence on the heart and circulation. *Artery Research, 1*, S7-S14. doi: 10.1016/S1872-9312(07)70002-9

Prioleau Jr., W. H., Parker, E. F., Bradham, R. R., & Gregorie Jr., H. (1976). Dirofilaria immitis (dog heartworm) as a pulmonary lesion in humans. *The Annals of Thoracic Surgery, 21*(5), 382-385. doi: 10.1016/S0003-4975(10)63884-2

Rawlings, C. A. (1986). *Heartworm disease in dogs and cats.* Philadelphia: Saunders.

Robin, E. D., Cross, C. E., & Zelis, R. (1973). Pulmonary edema. *New England Journal of Medicine, 288*(6), 292-304. doi: 10.1056/NEJM197302082880606

Sacks, B. N., & Caswell-Chen, E. P. (2003). Reconstructing the spread Of Dirofilaria immitis in California coyotess. *Journal of Parasitology, 89*(2), 319-323. doi: 10.1645/0022-3395(2003)089[0319:RTSODI]2.0.CO;2

Sasaki, Y., Kitagawa, H., Ishihara, K., & Masegi, T. (1990). Improvement in pulmonary arterial lesions after heartworm removal using flexible alligator forceps. *The Japanese Journal of Veterinary Science, 52*(4), 743-752. doi: 10.1292/jvms1939.52.743

Schafer, M., & Berry, C. R. (1995). Cardiac and pulmonary artery mensuration In feline heartworm disease. *Veterinary Radiology Ultrasound, 36*(6), 499-505. doi: 10.1111/j.1740-8261.1995.tb00302.x

Schaper, R., Heine, J., Arther, R. G., Charles, S. D., & McCall, J. (2007). Imidacloprid plus Moxidectin to prevent heartworm infection (Dirofilaria immitis) in ferrets. *Parasitology Research, 101*(S1), 57-62. doi: 10.1007/s00436-007-0611-y

Schober, K. E., Hart, T. M., Stern, J. A., Li, X., Samii, V. F., Zekas, L. J., ... Bonagura, J. D. (2011). Effects of treatment on respiratory rate, serum natriuretic peptide concentration, and Doppler echocardiographic indices of left ventricular filling pressure in dogs with congestive heart failure secondary to degenerative mitral valve disease and dilated cardiomyopathy. *Journal of the American Veterinary Medical Association, 239*(4), 468-479. doi: 10.2460/javma.239.4.468

Schuller, S., Van Israël, N., Vanbelle, S., Clercx, C., & McENTEE, K. (2010). Lack of efficacy of low-dose spironolactone as adjunct treatment to conventional congestive heart failure treatment in dogs. *Journal of Veterinary Pharmacology and Therapeutics*, No-No. doi: 10.1111/j.1365-2885.2010.01235.x

Serres, F., Nicolle, A. P., Tissier, R., Gouni, V., Pouchelon, J., & Chetboul, V. (2006). Efficacy of oral tadalafil, a new long-acting phosphodiesterase-5 Inhibitor, for the short-term treatment of pulmonary arterial hypertension in a dog. *Journal of Veterinary Medicine Series A, 53*(3), 129-133. doi: 10.1111/j.1439-0442.2006.00800.x

Sevimli, F. K., Kozan, E., Bülbül, A., Birdane, F. M., Köse, M., & Sevimli, A. (2007). Dirofilaria immitis infection in dogs: Unusually located and unusual findings. *Parasitology Research, 101*(6), 1487-1494. doi: 10.1007/s00436-007-0665-x

Simón, F., Kramer, L. H., Román, A., Blasini, W., Morchón, R., Marcos-Atxutegi, C., ... Genchi, C. (2007). Immunopathology of dirofilaria immitis infection. *Veterinary Research Communications, 31*(2), 161-171. doi: 10.1007/s11259-006-3387-0

Simo n, F., & Genchi, C. (2001). *Heartworm infection in humans and animals.* Salamanca: Ediciones Universidad de Salamanca.

Slappendel, R. J., Arkel, C. V., Mieog, W. W., & Bouma, B. N. (1972). Response to heparin of spontaneous disseminated intravascular coagulation in the dog. *Zentralblatt Für Veterinärmedizin Reihe A, 19*(6), 502-513. doi: 10.1111/j.1439-0442.1972.tb00501.x

Stockhaus, C., & Slappendel, R. J. (1998). Haemophagocytic syndrome with disseminated intravascular coagulation in a dog. *Journal of Small Animal Practice, 39*(4), 203-206. doi: 10.1111/j.1748-5827.1998.tb03632.x

Stokol, T., Brooks, M. B., Erb, H. N., & Mauldin, G. E. (2000). D-dimer concentrations in healthy dogs and dogs with disseminated intravascular coagulation. *American Journal of*

Veterinary Research, 61(4), 393-398. doi: 10.2460/ajvr.2000.61.393

Strickland, K. (1998). Canine and feline caval syndrome. *Clinical Techniques in Small Animal Practice, 13*(2), 88-95. doi: 10.1016/S1096-2867(98)80012-1

Supakorndej, P., Lewis, R. E., McCall, J. W., Dzimianski, M. T., & Holmes, R. A. (1995). Radiographic and angiographic evaluations of ferrets experimentally infected with dirofilaria immitis. *Veterinary Radiology, 36*(1), 23-29. doi: 10.1111/j.1740-8261.1995.tb00208.x

Sutton, R. H., & Atwell, R. B. (1985). Lesions of pulmonary pleura associated with canine heartworm disease. *Veterinary Pathology, 22*(6), 637-639. doi: 10.1177/030098588502200620

Suzuki, Y., Suu, S., & Satoh, H. (1970). Cerebrospinal lesions resulting from invasion of canine heartworm larvae. *The Japanese Journal of Veterinary Science, 32*(1), 11-17_2. doi: 10.1292/jvms1939.32.11

Tarish, J. H., & Atwell, R. B. (1993). The development of pulmonary lesions associated with dead adult D. immitis in naive dogs. *Journal of Veterinary Medicine, Series B, 40*(1-10), 197-205. doi: 10.1111/j.1439-0450.1993.tb00128.x

Tarnow, I., Falk, T., Tidholm, A., Martinussen, T., Jensen, A. L., Olsen, L. H., ... Kristensen, A. T. (2007). Hemostatic biomarkers in dogs with chronic congestive heart failure. *Journal of Veterinary Internal Medicine, 21*(3), 451. doi: 10.1892/0891-6640(2007)21[451:HBIDWC]2.0.CO;2

Wada, H. (2004). Disseminated intravascular coagulation. *Clinica Chimica Acta, 344*(1-2), 13-21. doi: 10.1016/S0009-8981(04)00101-9

Wagner, R. (2009). Ferret Cardiology. *Veterinary Clinics of North America: Exotic Animal Practice, 12*(1), 115-134. doi: 10.1016/j.cvex.2008.09.001

Wallace, C. R. (1965). Spontaneous congestive heart failure In the dog. *Annals of the New York Academy of Sciences, 127*(1 Comparative C), 570-580. doi: 10.1111/j.1749-6632.1965.tb49424.x

Wright, I. (2009). Feline heartworm: A threat to the travelling cat. *Companion Animal, 14*(9), 33-36. doi: 10.1111/j.2044-3862.2009.tb00423.x

Yilmaz, Z., Ozarda, Y., Cansev, M., Eralp, O., Kocaturk, M., & Ulus, I. H. (2010). Choline or CDP-choline attenuates coagulation abnormalities and prevents the development of acute disseminated intravascular coagulation in dogs during endotoxemia. *Blood Coagulation & Fibrinolysis, 21*(4), 339-348. doi: 10.1097/MBC.0b013e328338ce31

CHAPTER FIVE

Abraham, D., Leon, O., Leon, S., & Lustigman, S. (2001). Development of a recombinant antigen vaccine against infection with the filarial worm Onchocerca volvulus. *Infection and Immunity, 69*(1), 262-270. doi: 10.1128/IAI.69.1.262-270.2001

Ahid, S. M., Vasconcelos, P. S., & Lourenço-de-Oliveira, R. (2000). Vector competence of Culex quinquefasciatus say from different regions of Brazil to Dirofilaria immitis. *Memórias Do Instituto Oswaldo Cruz, 95*(6). doi: 10.1590/S0074-02762000000600004

Allen, J. E., Adjei, O., Bain, O., Hoerauf, A., Hoffmann, W. H., Makepeace, B. L., ... Taylor, D. W. (2008). Of mice, cattle, and humans: The immunology and treatment of river blindness (S. Lustigman, Ed.). *PLoS Neglected*

Tropical Diseases, 2(4), E217. doi: 10.1371/journal.pntd.0000217

Anastasia, U. (2010). Anti-carcinoma, anti-obesity, antidiabetic and immune defence effects of Vernonia amygdalina leaf extract and leaf powder, in two human cancer patients. *American Journal of Immunology.*

Anyanwu, I., Agbede, R., Ajanusi, O., Umoh, J., & Ibrahim, N. (2000). The incrimination of Aedes (stegomyia) aegypti as the vector of Dirofilaria repens in Nigeria. *Veterinary Parasitology, 92*(4), 319-327. doi: 10.1016/S0304-4017(00)00311-3

Beauperthuy on mosquito-born diseases. (1908). *Science, 28*(708), 114-114. doi: 10.1126/science.28.708.114

Becker, N. (2008). Influence of climate change on mosquito development and mosquito-borne diseases in Europe. *Parasitology Research, 103*(S1), 19-28. doi: 10.1007/s00436-008-1210-2

Benitez, M. A. (2009). Climate change could affect mosquito-borne diseases in Asia. *The Lancet, 373*(9669), 1070. doi: 10.1016/S0140-6736(09)60634-6

Brown, H., Harrington, L., Kaufman, P., McKay, T., Bowman, D., & Nelson, C. (2012). Key factors influencing canine heartworm, Dirofilaria immitis, in the United States. *Parasites & Vectors, 5*, 245.

Cameron, T. M. (1928). On the habitat of Ælurostrongylus abstrusus, the lung worm of the Cat. *Journal of Helminthology, 6*(03), 165. doi: 10.1017/S0022149X0002993X

Cancrini, G., Frangipane di Regalbono, A., Ricci, I., Tessarin, C., Gabrielli, S., & Pietrobelli, M. (2003). Aedes albopictus is a natural vector of Dirofilaria immitis in Italy. *Veterinary Parasitology, 118*(3-4), 195-202. doi: 10.1016/j.vetpar.2003.10.011

Carvalho, G. D., Alves, L. C., Maia, R. T., Andrade, C. D., Ramos, R. N., & Faustino, M. G. (2008). Vector competence of Culex quinquefasciatus Say, 1823 exposed to different densities of microfilariae of Dirofilaria immitis (Leidy, 1856). *Revista Brasileira De Entomologia, 52*(4). doi: 10.1590/S0085-56262008000400018

Christensen, B., & Hollander, A. (1978). Effect of temperature on vector-parasite relationships of Aedes trivittatus and Dirofilaria immitis. *Proceedings of the Helminthological Society of Washington, 45*, 115-119.

Clifton, J. (2007). *Stop the shots!: Are vaccinations killing our pets?* New York, NY: Foley Square Books.

Collins, D., & Cook, D. (2006). Laboratory studies evaluating the efficacy of diatomaceous earths, on treated surfaces, against stored-product insect and mite pests. *Journal of Stored Products Research, 42*(1), 51-60. doi: 10.1016/j.jspr.2004.09.002

Collins, J., Williams, J., & Kaiser, L. (1994). Dirofilaria immitis: Heartworm products contract rat trachea in vitro. *Exp Parasitol, 78*(1), 76-84.

Conboy, G. (2011). Canine angiostrongylosis: The French heartworm: An emerging threat in North America. *Veterinary Parasitology, 176*(4), 382-389. doi: 10.1016/j.vetpar.2011.01.025

Craster, C. V. (1921). Conquest of mosquito-borne diseases. *American Journal of Public Health, 11*(6), 538-543. doi: 10.2105/AJPH.11.6.538

Cupples, J. (2011). Wild globalization: The biopolitics of climate change and global capitalism on Nicaragua's Mosquito Coast. *Antipode*, No-No. doi: 10.1111/j.1467-8330.2010.00834.x

Debboun, M., Green, T. J., Rueda, L. M., & Hall, R. D. (2005). Relative abundance of tree hole–breeding mosquitoes in Boone county, Missouri, USA, with emphasis on the vector potential of Aedes triseriatus for canine heartworm, Dirofilaria immitis. *Journal of the American Mosquito Control Association, 21*(3), 274. doi: 10.2987/8756-971X(2005)21[274:RAOTHM]2.0.CO;2

Dereure, J., Vanwambeke, S. O., Malé, P., Martinez, S., Pratlong, F., Balard, Y., & Dedet, J. (2008). The potential effects of global warming on changes in canine Leishmaniasis in a focus outside the classical area of the disease in Southern France. *Vector-Borne and Zoonotic Diseases*, 090626040419041-8. doi: 10.1089/vbz.2008.0126

Dowling, P. (2006). Pharmacogenetics: It's not just about ivermectin in collies. *Can Vet J, 47*(12), 1165-1168.

Epstein, P. R., Diaz, H. F., Elias, S., Grabherr, G., Graham, N. E., Martens, W. M., ... Susskind, J. (1998). Biological and physical signs of climate change: Focus on mosquito-borne diseases. *Bulletin of the American Meteorological Society, 79*(3), 409-417. doi: 10.1175/1520-0477(1998)0792.0.CO;2

Ernst, J., & Slocombe, J. (1984). Mosquito vectors of *Dirofilaria immitis* in southwestern Ontario. *Canadian Journal of Zoology, 62*(2), 212-216. doi: 10.1139/z84-035

Ferdushy, T., & Hasan, M. T. (2010). Angiostrongylus vasorum: The 'French heartworm'. *Parasitology Research, 107*(4), 765-771. doi: 10.1007/s00436-010-2026-4

Frimeth, J. P., & Arai, H. P. (1983). Some potential mosquito vectors of the canine heartworm, Dirofilaria immitis, in the Calgary region of southern Alberta. *Canadian Journal of Zoology, 61*(5), 1156-1158. doi: 10.1139/z83-153

Gee, R. W., & Auty, J. H. (1957). The Heartworm Dirofilaria immitis in victoria.. *Australian Veterinary Journal, 33*(6), 152-153. doi: 10.1111/j.1751-0813.1957.tb08328.x

Genchi, C., Rinaldi, L., & Cringoli, G. (2007). ***Dirofilaria immitis and D. repens in dog and cat and human infections.*** Naples: Veterinary Parasitology and Parasitic Diseases, Dept. of Pathology and Animal Health, Faculty of Veterinary Medicine,University of Naples Federico II.

Genchi, C., Rinaldi, L., Cascone, C., Mortarino, M., & Cringoli, G. (2005). Is heartworm disease really spreading in Europe? *Veterinary Parasitology, 133*(2-3), 137-148. doi: 10.1016/j.vetpar.2005.04.009

Godel, C., Kumar, S., Koutsovoulos, G., Ludin, P., Nilsson, D., Comandatore, F., ... Mäser, P. (0006, May 03). Abstract. *National Center for Biotechnology Information.* Retrieved from ncbi.nlm.nih.gov/pmc/articles/PMC3475251/

González Canga, A., Sahagún Prieto, A. M., Diez Liébana, M. J., Fernández Martínez, N., Sierra Vega, M., & García Vieitez, J. J. (2008). The pharmacokinetics and interactions of ivermectin in humans—A mini-review. *The AAPS Journal, 10*(1), 42-46. doi: 10.1208/s12248-007-9000-9

Gould, F., Magori, K., & Huang, Y. (2006). Genetic strategies for controlling mosquito-borne diseases. *American Scientist, 94*(3), 238. doi: 10.1511/2006.3.238

Grandi, G., Quintavalla, C., Mavropoulou, A., Genchi, M., Gnudi, G., Bertoni, G., & Kramer, L. (2010). A combination of doxycycline and ivermectin is adulticidal in dogs with naturally acquired heartworm disease (Dirofilaria immitis). *Veterinary Parasitology, 169*(3-4), 347-351. doi: 10.1016/j.vetpar.2010.01.025

Grandi, G., Quintavalla, C., Mavropoulou, A., Genchi, M., Gnudi, G., Bertoni, G., & Kramer, L. (2011). Corrigendum to "A combination of doxycycline and ivermectin is adulticidal in dogs with naturally acquired heartworm disease (Dirofilaria immitis)" [Vet. Parasitol. 169 (2010) 347–351]. *Veterinary Parasitology, 177*(1-2), 196. doi: 10.1016/j.vetpar.2010.12.001

H., J. M. (1887). The sense of smell in dogs. *Nature, 36*(931), 412-412. doi: 10.1038/036412a0

Hoegh-Guldberg, O., Mumby, P. J., Hooten, A. J., Steneck, R. S., Greenfield, P., Gomez, E., ... Hatziolos, M. E. (2007). Coral reefs under rapid climate change and ocean acidification. *Science, 318*(5857), 1737-1742. doi: 10.1126/science.1152509

Hongoh, V., Berrang-Ford, L., Scott, M., & Lindsay, L. (2012). Expanding geographical distribution of the mosquito, Culex pipiens, in Canada under climate change. *Applied Geography, 33*, 53-62. doi: 10.1016/j.apgeog.2011.05.015

Houghton, J. (2005). Global warming. *Reports on Progress in Physics, 68*(6), 1343-1403. doi: 10.1088/0034-4885/68/6/R02

Hugnet, C., Bentjen, S. A., & Mealey, K. L. (2004). Frequency of the mutant MDR1 allele associated with multidrug sensitivity in a sample of collies from France. *Journal of Veterinary Pharmacology and Therapeutics, 27*(4), 227-229. doi: 10.1111/j.1365-2885.2004.00585.x

Hurlbert, S. H., Zedler, J., & Fairbanks, D. (1972). Ecosystem alteration by mosquitofish (Gambusia affinis) predation. *Science, 175*(4022), 639-641. doi: 10.1126/science.175.4022.639

Johnston-Lavis, H. J. (1880). Mosquitos. *Nature, 22*(570), 511-511. doi: 10.1038/022511c0

Kaiser, L. (1998). Dirofilaria immitis: Heartworm infection converts histamine-induced constriction to endothelium-dependent relaxation in canine pulmonary artery. *Experimental Parasitology, 88*(2), 146-153. doi: 10.1006/expr.1998.4219

Karl, T. R. (2003). Modern global climate change. *Science, 302*(5651), 1719-1723. doi: 10.1126/science.1090228

Khandekar, M. L., Murty, T. S., & Chittibabu, P. (2005). The global warming debate: A review of the state of science. *Pure and Applied Geophysics, 162*(8-9), 1557-1586. doi: 10.1007/s00024-005-2683-x

Kitoh, K., Katoh, H., Kitagawa, H., Nagase, M., Sasaki, N., & Sasaki, Y. (2001). Role of histamine in heartworm extract-induced shock in dogs. *American Journal of Veterinary Research, 62*(5), 770-774. doi: 10.2460/ajvr.2001.62.770

Knight, D., & Lok, J. (1998). Seasonality of heartworm infection and implications for chemoprophylaxis. *Clinical Techniques in Small Animal Practice, 13*(2), 77-82. doi: 10.1016/S1096-2867(98)80010-8

Koneswaran, G., & Nierenberg, D. (2008). Global farm animal production and global warming: Impacting and mitigating climate change. *Environmental Health Perspectives.* doi: 10.1289/ehp.11034

Laaksonen, S., Pusenius, J., Kumpula, J., Venäläinen, A., Kortet, R., Oksanen, A., & Hoberg, E. (2010). Climate change promotes the emergence of serious disease outbreaks of filarioid nematodes. *EcoHealth, 7*(1), 7-13. doi: 10.1007/s10393-010-0308-z

Labarthe, N., Serrão, M. L., Melo, Y. F., Oliveira, S. D., & Lourenço-de-Oliveira, R. (1998). Potential vectors of Dirofilaria immitis (Leidy, 1856) in Itacoatiara, oceanic region of Niterói municipality, state of Rio de Janeiro, Brazil. *Memórias Do Instituto Oswaldo Cruz, 93*(4). doi: 10.1590/S0074-02761998000400001

Lai, C., & Putnak, R. (2006). Dengue and the dengue viruses. *Perspectives in Medical Virology, 16*, 269-298. doi: 10.1016/S0168-7069(06)16011-5

Lima, C. L., Freitas, F. S., Morais, L. D., Cavalcanti, M. S., Silva, L. D., Padilha, R. R., ... Diniz, M. M. (2011). Ultrastructural study on the morphological changes to male worms of Schistosoma mansoni after in vitro exposure to allicin. *Revista Da Sociedade Brasileira De Medicina Tropical, 44*(3), 327-330. doi: 10.1590/S0037-86822011005000023

Lipkowitz, M. A., & Navarra, T. (2001). *Encyclopedia of allergies*. New York, NY: Facts On File.

Manrique-Saide, P., Escobedo-Ortegón, J., Bolio-González, M., Sauri-Arceo, C., Dzib-Florez, S., Guillermo-May, G., ... Lenhart, A. (2010). Incrimination of the mosquito, Aedes taeniorhynchus, as the primary vector of heartworm, Dirofilaria immitis, in coastal Yucatan, Mexico. *Medical and Veterinary Entomology, 24*(4), 456-460. doi: 10.1111/j.1365-2915.2010.00884.x

Mattingly, P. F. (1983). The palaeogeography of mosquito-borne disease. *Biological Journal of the Linnean Society, 19*(2), 185-210. doi: 10.1111/j.1095-8312.1983.tb00783.x

Mazzariol, S., Cassini, R., Voltan, L., Aresu, L., & Frangipane di Regalbono, A. (2010). Heartworm (Dirofilaria immitis) infection in a leopard (Panthera pardus pardus) housed in a zoological park in north-eastern Italy. *Parasites & Vectors, 3*(1), 25. doi: 10.1186/1756-3305-3-25

Mealey, K. L., Bentjen, S. A., & Waiting, D. K. (2002). Frequency of the mutant MDR1 allele associated with ivermectin sensitivity in a sample population of Collies from the northwestern United States. *American Journal of Veterinary Research, 63*(4), 479-481. doi: 10.2460/ajvr.2002.63.479

Müller, G. C., Beier, J. C., Traore, S. F., Toure, M. B., Traore, M. M., Bah, S., ... Schlein, Y. (2010). Successful field trial of attractive toxic sugar bait (ATSB) plant-spraying methods against malaria vectors in the Anopheles gambiae complex in Mali, West Africa. *Malaria Journal, 9*(1), 210. doi: 10.1186/1475-2875-9-210

Müller, G. C., Junnila, A., Qualls, W., Revay, E. E., Kline, D. L., Allan, S., ... Xue, R. D. (2010). Control of Culex quinquefasciatus in a storm drain system in Florida using attractive toxic sugar baits. *Medical and Veterinary Entomology, 24*(4), 346-351. doi: 10.1111/j.1365-2915.2010.00876.x

Müller, G. C., Kravchenko, V. D., & Schlein, Y. (2008). Decline of Anopheles sergentii and Aedes caspius populations following presentation of attractive toxic (Spinosad) sugar bait stations in an oasis. *Journal of the American Mosquito Control Association, 24*(1), 147-149. doi: 10.2987/8756-971X(2008)24[147:DOASAA]2.0.CO;2

Morchón, R., Carretón, E., González-Miguel, J., & Mellado-Hernández, I. (2012, June 12). Abstract. *National Center for Biotechnology Information*. Retrieved from ncbi.nlm.nih.gov/pmc/articles/PMC3372948/

Morin, C. W., & Comrie, A. C. (2010). Modeled response of the West Nile virus vector Culex quinquefasciatus to changing climate using the dynamic mosquito simulation model. *International Journal of Biometeorology, 54*(5), 517-529. doi: 10.1007/s00484-010-0349-6

Nagano, I. (1996). A simple method to design PCR primer to detect genomic DNA of parasites and its application toDirofilaria immitis. *Molecular and Cellular Probes, 10*(6), 423-425. doi: 10.1006/mcpr.1996.0058

New Jersey mosquito biology and control. Center for vector biology. (1996, July). *New Jersey Mosquito Biology and Control.*

Center for Vector Biology. Retrieved from rci.rutgers.edu/~insects/mosfaq.htm

O'Shaughnessy, P. T. (2008). Parachuting cats and crushed eggs the controversy over the use of DDT to control malaria. *American Journal of Public Health, 98*(11), 1940-1948. doi: 10.2105/AJPH.2007.122523

Otto, G. (1969). Geographical distribution, vectors and life cycle of Dirofilaria immitis. *Journal of the American Veterinary Medical Association, 154*, 370-373.

Paaijmans, K. P., Imbahale, S. S., Thomas, M. B., & Takken, W. (2010). Relevant microclimate for determining the development rate of malaria mosquitoes and possible implications of climate change. *Malaria Journal, 9*(1), 196. doi: 10.1186/1475-2875-9-196

Patz, J. A. (2006). Malaria risk and temperature: Influences from global climate change and local land use practices. *Proceedings of the National Academy of Sciences, 103*(15), 5635-5636. doi: 10.1073/pnas.0601493103

Platonov, A. E., Fedorova, M. V., Karan, L. S., Shopenskaya, T. A., Platonova, O. V., & Zhuravlev, V. I. (2008). Epidemiology of west nile infection in Volgograd, Russia, in relation to climate change and mosquito (Diptera: Culicidae) bionomics. *Parasitology Research, 103*(S1), 45-53. doi: 10.1007/s00436-008-1050-0

Plumb, J. (1981). Lung worms in dogs. *Veterinary Record, 109*(12), 267-268. doi: 10.1136/vr.109.12.267

Reiter, P. (2008). Global warming and malaria: Knowing the horse before hitching the cart. *Malaria Journal, 7*(Suppl 1), S3. doi: 10.1186/1475-2875-7-S1-S3

A report on the risk to NZ of canine heartworm (Dirofilaria immitis) and quarantine measures which could be considered appropria. (2008, April 30). *Welcome to MPI Biosecurity New Zealand.* Retrieved from biosecurity.govt.nz/pests-diseases/animals/risk/dirofilaria-immitis.htm

Reppert, B. (2006). Global warming: Congress still stalled, states and cities act. *BioScience, 56*(10), 800. doi: 10.1641/0006-3568(2006)56[800:GWCSSS]2.0.CO;2

Rinaldi, L., Genchi, C., Musella, V., Genchi, M., & Cringoli, G. (2011). Geographical information systems as a tool in the control of heartworm infections in dogs and cats. *Veterinary Parasitology, 176*(4), 286-290. doi: 10.1016/j.vetpar.2011.01.010

Root, T. L., Price, J. T., Hall, K. R., Schneider, S. H., Rosenzweig, C., & Pounds, J. A. (2003). Fingerprints of global warming on wild animals and plants. *Nature, 421*(6918), 57-60. doi: 10.1038/nature01333

Russell R. (1985). Report of a field study on mosquito (Diptera: Culicidae) vectors of dog heartworm, Dirofilaria immitis Leidy (Spirurida: Onchocercidae) near Sydney, N.s.w., and the implications for veterinary and public health concern. *Australian Journal of Zoology, 33*(4), 461. doi: 10.1071/ZO9850461

Russell, R. C., & Geary, M. J. (1992). The susceptibility of the mosquitoes Aedes notoscriptus and Culex annulirostris to infection with dog heartworm Dirofilaria immitis and their vector efficiency. *Medical and Veterinary Entomology, 6*(2), 154-158. doi: 10.1111/j.1365-2915.1992.tb00594.x

Russell, R. C. (2009). Climate change and mosquito-borne disease: Likely impacts in australia. *Pathology, 41*(Sup 1), 47. doi: 10.1097/01268031-200941001-00098

Russell, R. C. (2009). Mosquito-borne disease and climate change in Australia: Time for a reality check. *Australian Journal of Entomology, 48*(1), 1-7. doi: 10.1111/j.1440-6055.2008.00677.x

Sacks, B. N., & Caswell-Chen, E. P. (2003). Reconstructing the spread of Dirofilaria immitis in California coyotes. *Journal of Parasitology, 89*(2), 319-323. doi: 10.1645/0022-3395(2003)089[0319:RTSODI]2.0.CO;2

Saint-Marie, E., & Ducos, D. L. (2003). *Mise au point sur l'angiostrongylose canine the□rapeutique actuelle.* [S.l.]: [s.n.].

Schaper, R., Heine, J., Arther, R. G., Charles, S. D., & McCall, J. (2007). Imidacloprid plus Moxidectin to Prevent Heartworm Infection (Dirofilaria immitis) in Ferrets. *Parasitology Research, 101*(S1), 57-62. doi: 10.1007/s00436-007-0611-y

Sevimli, F. K., Kozan, E., Bülbül, A., Birdane, F. M., Köse, M., & Sevimli, A. (2007). Dirofilaria immitis infection in dogs: Unusually located and unusual findings. *Parasitology Research, 101*(6), 1487-1494. doi: 10.1007/s00436-007-0665-x

Simo n, F., & Genchi, C. (2001). *Heartworm infection in humans and animals.* Salamanca: Ediciones Universidad de Salamanca.

Symes, C. B. (1960). A Note on Dirofilaria immitis and its vectors in Fiji. *Journal of Helminthology, 34*(1-2), 39. doi: 10.1017/S0022149X00020319

Tariq, M. (2008). Nigella sativa seeds: Folklore treatment in modern medicine. *Saudi Journal of Gastroenterology, 14*(3), 105. doi: 10.4103/1319-3767.41725

Tebb, A., Johnson, V., & Irwin, P. (2007). Angiostrongylus vasorum (French heartworm) in a dog imported into Australia. *Australian Veterinary Journal, 85*(1-2), 23-28. doi: 10.1111/j.1751-0813.2006.00085.x

Tolle, M. A. (2009). Mosquito-borne diseases. *Current Problems in Pediatric and Adolescent Health Care, 39*(4), 97-140. doi: 10.1016/j.cppeds.2009.01.001

Traversa, D., Di Cesare, A., & Conboy, G. (2010). Canine and feline cardiopulmonary parasitic nematodes in Europe: Emerging and underestimated. *Parasites & Vectors, 3*(1), 62. doi: 10.1186/1756-3305-3-62

Trpiš, M., Haufe, W., & Shemanchuk, J. (1968). Mermithid parasites of the mosquito *Aedes vexans* Meigen in British Columbia. *Canadian Journal of Zoology, 46*(5), 1077-1079. doi: 10.1139/z68-150

Wagner, R. (2009). Ferret Cardiology. *Veterinary Clinics of North America: Exotic Animal Practice, 12*(1), 115-134. doi: 10.1016/j.cvex.2008.09.001

Walther, G., Post, E., Convey, P., Menzel, A., Parmesan, C., Beebee, T. C., ... Bairlein, F. (2002). Ecological responses to recent climate change. *Nature, 416*(6879), 389-395. doi: 10.1038/416389a

Watson, R. (2003). 8 reasons why spraying pesticides is not the solution to wnv. *8 Reasons Why Spraying Pesticides Is Not the Solution to Wnv.* Retrieved from environmentalhealth.ca/spring03false.html

Weissenböck, H., Hubálek, Z., Bakonyi, T., & Nowotny, N. (2010). Zoonotic mosquito-borne flaviviruses: Worldwide presence of agents with proven pathogenicity and potential candidates of future emerging diseases. *Veterinary Microbiology, 140*(3-4), 271-280. doi: 10.1016/j.vetmic.2009.08.025

White, E. P. (2004). Factors affecting bat house occupancy in Colorado (C. A. Jones, Ed.). *The Southwestern Naturalist, 49*(3), 344-349. doi: 10.1894/0038-4909(2004)0492.0.CO;2

Wong, S. S., Teng, J. L., Poon, R. W., Choi, G. K., Chan, K., Yeung, M. L., ... Yuen, K. (2011). Comparative evaluation of a point-of-care immunochromatographic test SNAP 4Dx with molecular detection tests for vector-borne canine pathogens in Hong Kong. *Vector-Borne and Zoonotic Diseases, 11*(9), 1269-1277. doi: 10.1089/vbz.2010.0265

Yildirim, A., Inci, A., Duzlu, O., Biskin, Z., Ica, A., & Sahin, I. (2011). Aedes vexans and Culex pipiens as the potential vectors of Dirofilaria immitis in Central Turkey. *Veterinary Parasitology, 178*(1-2), 143-147. doi: 10.1016/j.vetpar.2010.12.023

Zaoui, A., Cherrah, Y., Mahassini, N., Alaoui, K., Amarouch, H., & Hassar, M. (2002). Acute and chronic toxicity of Nigella sativa fixed oil. *Phytomedicine, 9*(1), 69-74.

CHAPTER SIX

Abuelgasim, A., Omer, E., & Elmahdi, B. (2008). The effectiveness of Nigella sativa against liver damage in rats. *Research Journal of Medicinal Plant, 2*(1), 43-47. doi: 10.3923/rjmp.2008.43.47

Al-Hader, A., Aqel, M., & Hasan, Z. (1993). Hypoglycemic effects of the volatile oil of Nigella sativa seeds. *Pharmaceutical Biology, 31*(2), 96-100. doi: 10.3109/13880209309082925

Ali, Z., & Khan, I. (2008). Chemical constituents of Nigella sative (Black cumin). *Planta Medica, 74*(03). doi: 10.1055/s-2008-1075306

Aqel, M. B. (1993). Effects of Nigella sativa seeds on intestinal smooth muscle. *Pharmaceutical Biology, 31*(1), 55-60. doi: 10.3109/13880209309082918

Araneda, R. C. (2004). The scents of androstenone in humans. *The Journal of Physiology, 554*(1), 1-1. doi: 10.1113/jphysiol.2003.057075

Arther, R., Charles, S., Ciszewski, D., Davis, W., & Settje, T. (2005). Imidacloprid/moxidectin topical solution for the prevention of heartworm disease and the treatment and control of flea and intestinal nematodes of cats. *Veterinary Parasitology, 133*(2-3), 219-225. doi: 10.1016/j.vetpar.2005.04.001

Arther, R. G., Atkins, C., Ciszewski, D. K., Davis, W. L., Ensley, S. M., & Settje, T. L. (2005). Safety of imidacloprid plus moxidectin topical solution applied to cats heavily infected with adult heartworms (Dirofilaria immitis). *Parasitology Research, 97*(S01), S70-S75. doi: 10.1007/s00436-005-1447-y

Arther, R. G., Bowmann, D. D., McCall, J. W., Hansen, O., & Young, D. R. (2003). Feline advantage heart? (imidacloprid and moxidectin) topical solution as monthly treatment for prevention of heartworm infection (Dirofilaria immitis) and control of fleas (Ctenocephalides felis) on cats. *Parasitology Research, 90*(0), S137-S139. doi: 10.1007/s00436-003-0917-3

Atkins, C., Moresco, A., & Litster, A. (2005). Prevalence of naturally occurring Dirofilaria immitis infection among nondomestic cats housed in an area in which heartworms are endemic. *Journal of the American Veterinary Medical Association, 227*(1), 139-143. doi: 10.2460/javma.2005.227.139

Atwell, R., & Tarish, J. H. (1995). The effect of oral, low-dose prednisolone on the extent of pulmonary pathology associated with dead Dirofilaria immitis in a canine lung model. *Proceedings of the Heartworm Symposium '95*, 103-111.

Atwell, R. (1988). Basic pathophysiology and epidemiology of heartworm disease in Australia. *Heartworm Symposium, 36.*

Atwell, R. (1992). Dirofilaria immitis in cats. *Australian Veterinary Journal, 69*(2), 44-44. doi: 10.1111/j.1751-0813.1992.tb07440.x

Bandi, C., Mccall, J., Genchi, C., Corona, S., Venco, L., & Sacchi, L. (1999). Effects of tetracycline on the filarial worms Brugia pahangi and Dirofilaria immitis and their bacterial endosymbionts Wolbachia. *International Journal for Parasitology, 29*(2), 357-364. doi: 10.1016/S0020-7519(98)00200-8

Baneth, G., Volansky, Z., Anug, Y., Favia, G., Bain, O., Goldstein, R. E., & Harrus, S. (2002). Dirofilaria repens infection in a dog: Diagnosis and treatment with melarsomine and doramectin. *Veterinary Parasitology, 105*(2), 173-178. doi: 10.1016/S0304-4017(02)00006-7

Bazzocchi, C., Mortarino, M., Grandi, G., Kramer, L., Genchi, C., Bandi, C., ... McCall, J. (2008). Combined ivermectin and doxycycline treatment has microfilaricidal and adulticidal activity against Dirofilaria immitis in experimentally infected dogs. *International Journal for Parasitology, 38*(12), 1401-1410. doi: 10.1016/j.ijpara.2008.03.002

Bazzocchi, C., Mortarino, M., Grandi, G., Kramer, L., Genchi, C., Bandi, C., ... McCall, J. (2008). Combined ivermectin and doxycycline treatment has microfilaricidal and adulticidal activity against Dirofilaria immitis in experimentally infected dogs. *International Journal for Parasitology, 38*(12), 1401-1410. doi: 10.1016/j.ijpara.2008.03.002

Block, E., Ahmad, S., Jain, M. K., Crecely, R. W., Apitz-Castro, R., & Cruz, M. R. (1984). The chemistry of alkyl thiosulfate esters. 8. (E,Z)-Ajoene: A potent antithrombotic agent from garlic. *Journal of the American Chemical Society, 106*(26), 8295-8296. doi: 10.1021/ja00338a049

Boudreaux, M. K., Dillon, A. R., Ravis, W. R., Sartin, E. A., & Spano, J. S. (1991). Effects of treatment with aspirin or aspirin/dipyridamole combination in heartworm-negative, heartworm-infected, and embolized heartworm-infected dogs. *Am J Vet Res, 52*(12), 1992-1999.

Bratton, R. L., Whiteside, J. W., Hovan, M. J., Engle, R. L., & Edwards, F. D. (2008). Diagnosis and treatment of Lyme disease. *Mayo Clinic Proceedings, 83*(5), 566-571. doi: 10.4065/83.5.566

Busby, J. L. (2005). *How to afford veterinary care without mortgaging the kids: Common sense and money saving advice from an old, country vet.* Bemidji, MN: Old Country Vet.

Caldin, M., Carli, E., Furlanello, T., Solano-Gallego, L., Tasca, S., Patron, C., & Lubas, G. (2005). A retrospective study of 60 cases of eccentrocytosis in the dog. *Veterinary Clinical Pathology, 34*(3), 224-231. doi: 10.1111/j.1939-165X.2005.tb00045.x

Campbell, W., Blair, L., & McCall, J. (1979). Brugia pahangi and Dirofilaria immitis: Experimental infections in the ferret, Mustela putorius furo. *Experimental Parasitology, 47*(3), 327-332. doi: 10.1016/0014-4894(79)90085-7

Carlisle, C. H. (1970). The experimental production of heartworm disease in the dog. *Australian Veterinary Journal, 46*(5), 190-194. doi: 10.1111/j.1751-0813.1970.tb01999.x

Carlisle, C. H., Prescott, C. W., McCosker, P. J., & Seawright, A. A. (1974). The toxic effects of thiacetarsamide sodium in normal dogs and in dogs infested with dirofilaria immitis. *Australian Veterinary Journal, 50*(5), 204-208. doi: 10.1111/j.1751-0813.1974.tb02365.x

Collins, G. H., & Pope, S. E. (1987). An evaluation of an ELISA test for the detection of antigens of Dirofilaria immitis. *Australian Veterinary Journal, 64*(10), 318-319. doi: 10.1111/j.1751-0813.1987.tb07342.x

Cottrell, D. (n.d.). Moxidectin As Heartworm Adulticide. *Moxidectin As Heartworm Adulticide.* Retrieved from weah4.tripod.com/id57.html

Courtney, C. H., & Zeng, Q. (2001). Comparison of heartworm antigen test kit performance in dogs having low heartworm burdens. *Veterinary Parasitology, 96*(4), 317-322. doi: 10.1016/S0304-4017(01)00374-0

Datta, S., Maitra, S., Gayen, P., & Sinha Babu, S. P. (2009). Improved efficacy of tetracycline by acaciasides on Dirofilaria immitis. *Parasitology Research, 105*(3), 697-702. doi: 10.1007/s00436-009-1441-x

Davidson, B. L., Rozanski, E. A., Tidwell, A. S., & Hoffman, A. M. (2006). Pulmonary thromboembolism in a heartworm-positive cat. *Journal of Veterinary Internal Medicine, 20*(4), 1037. doi: 10.1892/0891-6640(2006)20[1037:PTIAHC]2.0.CO;2

Dingman, P., Levy, J. K., Kramer, L. H., Johnson, C. M., Lappin, M. R., Greiner, E. C., ... Morchon, R. (2010). Association of Wolbachia with heartworm disease in cats and dogs. *Veterinary Parasitology, 170*(1-2), 50-60. doi: 10.1016/j.vetpar.2010.01.037

Ehrenberg, J. P., Tamashiro, W. K., & Scott, A. L. (1987). Dirofilaria immitis: Identification and characterization of circulating parasite antigens. *Experimental Parasitology, 63*(2), 205-214. doi: 10.1016/0014-4894(87)90163-9

Feinman, S. E. (1994). *Beneficial and toxic effects of aspirin.* Boca Raton: CRC Press.

Freeman, F., & Kodera, Y. (1995). Garlic chemistry: Stability of S-(2-Propenyl)-2-Propene-1-sulfinothioate (allicin) in blood, Solvents, and simulated physiological fluids. *Journal of Agricultural and Food Chemistry, 43*(9), 2332-2338. doi: 10.1021/jf00057a004

Fujisawa, H., Suma, K., Origuchi, K., Kumagai, H., Seki, T., & Ariga, T. (2008). Biological and chemical stability of garlic-derived allicin. *Journal of Agricultural and Food Chemistry, 56*(11), 4229-4235. doi: 10.1021/jf8000907

Gilani, A., Jabeen, Q., & Khan, M. (2004). A review of medicinal uses and pharmacological activities of Nigella sativa. *Pakistan Journal of Biological Sciences, 7*(4), 441-451. doi: 10.3923/pjbs.2004.441.451

Grandi, G., Quintavalla, C., Mavropoulou, A., Genchi, M., Gnudi, G., Bertoni, G., & Kramer, L. (2010). A combination of doxycycline and ivermectin is adulticidal in dogs with naturally acquired heartworm disease (Dirofilaria immitis). *Veterinary Parasitology, 169*(3-4), 347-351. doi: 10.1016/j.vetpar.2010.01.025

Grandi, G., Quintavalla, C., Mavropoulou, A., Genchi, M., Gnudi, G., Bertoni, G., & Kramer, L. (2011). Corrigendum to A combination of doxycycline and ivermectin is adulticidal in dogs with naturally acquired heartworm disease (Dirofilaria immitis) [Vet. Parasitol. 169 (2010) 347 351]. *Veterinary Parasitology, 177*(1-2), 196. doi: 10.1016/j.vetpar.2010.12.001

Greene, C. E. (1985). Effects of aspirin and propranolol on feline platelet aggregation. *Am J Vet Res, 46*, 1-4.

Hajhashemi, V., Ghannadi, A., & Jafarabadi, H. (2004). Black cumin seed essential oil, as a potent analgesic and antiin ammatory drug. *Phytotherapy*

Research, 18(3), 195-199. doi: 10.1002/ptr.1390

Hamilton, R. G., Scott, A. L., D'Antonio, R., Levy, D. A., & Adkinson Jr., N. (1983). Dirofilaria immitis: Performance and standardization of specific antibody immunoassays for filariasis. *Experimental Parasitology, 56*(3), 298-313. doi: 10.1016/0014-4894(83)90075-9

Islam, N., & Ansari, I. A. (2008). Beneficial role of allicin from garlic in cervical cancer. *Nature Precedings*. doi: 10.1038/npre.2008.1561.1

Jung, J., Chang, J., Oh, S., Yoon, J., & Choi, M. (2010). Computed tomography angiography for evaluation of pulmonary embolism in an experimental model and heartworm infested dogs. *Veterinary Radiology & Ultrasound, 51*(3), 288-293. doi: 10.1111/j.1740-8261.2009.01659.x

Keith, J. C., Rawlings, C. A., & Schaub, R. G. (1983). Pulmonary thromboembolism during therapy of dirofilariasis with thiacetarsamide: Modification with aspirin or prednisolone. *Am J Vet Res, 44*, 1278-1283.

Klasinc, L., Kova?, B., Sablji?, A., & McGlynn, S. P. (1987). Photoelectron spectroscopy of biologically active molecules. 14. Some analgesic-antipyretic and anti-inflammatory agents. *International Journal of Quantum Chemistry, 32*(S14), 317-324. doi: 10.1002/qua.560320828

Kolosov, M. N., Dobrynin, V. N., Gurevich, A. I., & Karapetyan, M. G. (1963). Tetracyclines. *Bulletin of the Academy of Sciences, USSR Division of Chemical Science, 12*(4), 622-626. doi: 10.1007/BF00843953

Kramer, L., Grandi, G., Passeri, B., Gianelli, P., Genchi, M., Dzimianski, M., ... McCall, J. (2011). Evaluation of lung pathology in Dirofilaria immitis-experimentally infected dogs treated with doxycycline or a combination of doxycycline and ivermectin before administration of melarsomine dihydrochloride. *Veterinary Parasitology, 176*(4), 357-360. doi: 10.1016/j.vetpar.2011.01.021

Lawson, L. D., & Wang, Z. J. (2001). Low allicin release from garlic supplements: A major problem due to the sensitivities of alliinase activity. *Journal of Agricultural and Food Chemistry, 49*(5), 2592-2599. doi: 10.1021/jf001287m

Lee, K., Yamato, O., Tajima, M., Kuraoka, M., Omae, S., & Maede, Y. (2000). Hematologic changes associated with the appearance of eccentrocytes after intragastric administration of garlic extract to dogs. *American Journal of Veterinary Research, 61*(11), 1446-1450. doi: 10.2460/ajvr.2000.61.1446

Lefkaditis, M., Koukeri, S., & Cozma, V. (2010). An endemic area of Dirofilaria immitis seropositive dogs at the eastern foothills of Mt Olympus, Northern Greece. *Helminthologia, 47*(1), 3-7. doi: 10.2478/s11687-010-0001-3

Litster, A., Atkins, C., & Atwell, R. (2008). Acute death in heartworm-infected cats: Unraveling the puzzle. *Veterinary Parasitology, 158*(3), 196-203. doi: 10.1016/j.vetpar.2008.09.007

Lorentzen, L., & Caola, A. E. (2008). Incidence of positive heartworm antibody and antigen tests at IDEXX Laboratories: Trends and potential impact on feline heartworm awareness and prevention. *Veterinary Parasitology, 158*(3), 183-190. doi: 10.1016/j.vetpar.2008.09.006

Maksimowich, D. S., Williams, J. F., & Kaiser, L. (1996). Thiacetarsamide depresses relaxation of canine pulmonary artery in vitro. *Veterinary Parasitology, 64*(3), 251-256. doi: 10.1016/0304-4017(95)00921-3

Mayer, J. (2013). *Clinical veterinary advisor: Birds and exotic pets.* Edinburgh: Saunders.

McCall, J., Kramer, L., Genchi, C., Guerrero, J., Dzimianski, M., Supakorndej, P., ... Carson, B. (2011). Effects of doxycycline on early infections of Dirofilaria immitis in dogs. *Veterinary Parasitology, 176*(4), 361-367. doi: 10.1016/j.vetpar.2011.01.022

McCall, J. W., McTier, T. L., Dzimianski, M. T., Raynaud, J., & Holmes, R. A. (1994). Clinical prophylactic activity of melarsomine dihydrochloride (RM 340) against Dirofilaria immitis in heartworm-naive beagles exposed to natural infection in three southeastern states. *Veterinary Parasitology, 55*(3), 205-219. doi: 10.1016/0304-4017(93)00642-C

McTier, T. L., McCall, J. W., Dzimianski, M. T., Raynaud, J., & Strickland, J. E. (1994). Use of melarsomine dihydrochloride (RM 340) for adulticidal treatment of dogs with naturally acquired infections of Dirofilaria immitis and for clinical prophylaxis during reexposure for 1 year. *Veterinary Parasitology, 55*(3), 221-233. doi: 10.1016/0304-4017(93)00643-D

Menounos, P., Staphylakis, K., & Gegiou, D. (1986). The sterols of Nigella sativa seed oil. *Phytochemistry, 25*(3), 761-763. doi: 10.1016/0031-9422(86)88046-3

Mullins, E. (1988). *Murder by injection: The story of the medical conspiracy against America.* Staunton, Va. (P.O. Box 1105, Staunton 24401): National Council for Medical Research.

Pitcairn, R. H., & Pitcairn, S. H. (2005). *Dr. Pitcairn's complete guide to natural health for dogs & cats.* [Emmaus, Pa.]: Rodale.

Rahman, M. S. (2007). Allicin and other functional active components in garlic: Health benefits and bioavailability. *International Journal of Food Properties, 10*(2), 245-268. doi: 10.1080/10942910601113327

Rawlings, C. A. (1986). *Heartworm disease in dogs and cats.* Philadelphia: Saunders.

Rawlings, C. A. (1990). Pulmonary arteriography and hemodynamics during feline heartworm disease. Effect of aspirin. *J Vet Intern Med, 4*(6), 286-291.

Rawlings, C. A., Farrell, R. L., & Mahood, R. M. (1990). Morphologic changes in the lungs of cats experimentally infected with Dirofilaria immitis. Response to aspirin. *J Vet Intern Med, 4*(6), 292-300.

Rawlings, C. A., Keith, J. C., & Schaub, R. G. (1985). Effect of acetylsalicylic acid on pulmonary arteriosclerosis induced by a 1 year, low level vascular injury. *Arteriosclerosis, 5*, 355-365.

Rawlings, C. A., Keith, J. C., & Schaub, R. G. (1985). Effect of acetylsalicylic acid on pulmonary arteriosclerosis induced by a one-year Dirofilaria immitis infection. *Arteriosclerosis, 5*, 355-365.

Rawlings, C. A., Keith, J. C., Losonsky, J. M., & Et al. (1983). Aspirin and prednisolone modification of post-adulticide pulmonary arterial disease in heartworm infection: Arteriographic study. *Am J Vet Res, 44*, 821-827.

Rawlings, C. A., Keith, J. C., Losonsky, J. M., & McCall, J. M. (1984). An aspirin-prednisolone combination to modify postadulticide lung disease in heartworm-infected dogs. *Am J Vet Res, 45*, 2371-2375.

Rawlings, C. A., Schaub, R. G., & Keith, J. C. (1984). The effect of acetylsalicylic acid on vascular damage and myointimal proliferation in canine pulmonary arteries subjected to chronic injury by Dirofilaria immitis infection. *68th Annu Meet Fed Proc.*

Rawlings, R. A., Schaub, R. G., & Keith, J. C. (1984). Aspirin reduces pulmonary arterial arteriosclerosis due to chronic vascular injury. *68th Annu Meet Fed Proc.*

Rossi, M. D., Paiva, J., Bendas, A., Mendes-de-Almeida, F., Knackfuss, F., Miranda, M., ... Labarthe, N. (2010). Effects of doxycycline on the endosymbiont Wolbachia in Dirofilaria immitis (Leidy, 1856) Naturally infected dogs. *Veterinary Parasitology, 174*(1-2), 119-123. doi: 10.1016/j.vetpar.2010.07.019

Salomi, N., Nair, S., Jayawardhanan, K., Varghese, C., & Panikkar, K. (1992). Antitumour principles from Nigella sativa seeds. *Cancer Letters, 63*(1), 41-46. doi: 10.1016/0304-3835(92)90087-C

Sardari, K., Dehgan, M. M., Mohri, M., Emami, M. R., Mirshahi, A., Maleki, M., ... Aslani, M. R. (2006). Macroscopic aspects of wound healing (contraction and epithelialisation) after topical administration of allicin in dogs. *Comparative Clinical Pathology, 15*(4), 231-235. doi: 10.1007/s00580-006-0634-2

Schaper, R., Heine, J., Arther, R. G., Charles, S. D., & McCall, J. (2007). Imidacloprid plus Moxidectin to prevent heartworm Infection (Dirofilaria immitis) in ferrets. *Parasitology Research, 101*(S1), 57-62. doi: 10.1007/s00436-007-0611-y

Schaub, R. G., Keith, J. C., & Rawlings, C. A. (1981). Effect of long-term aspirin treatment on platelet adhesion to chronically damaged canine pulmonary arteries. *Thromb Haemostasis, 46*, 680-683.

Schaub, R. G., Keith, J. C., Simmons, C. A., & Rawlings, C. A. (1985). Smooth muscle proliferation in chronically injured canine pulmonary arteries is reduced by a potent platelet aggregation inhibitor U-53,059. *Thromb Haemostasis, 53*, 351-355.

Schaub, R. G., Rawlings, C. A., & Keith, J. C. (1981). Effect of long-term aspirin treatment on platelet adhesion to chronically damaged canine pulmonary arteries. *Thromb Haemostasis, 46*, 680-683.

Schaub, R. G., Rawlings, C. A., & Keith, J. C. (1981). Platelet adhesion and myointimal proferation in canine pulmonary arteries. *Am J Pathol, 104*, 13-22.

Schleicher, P., & Saleh, M. (2000). ***Black cumin: The magical Egyptian herb for allergies, asthma, and immune disorders.*** Rochester, VT: Healing Arts Press.

Scott, A. L., Diala, C., Moraga, D. A., Ibrahim, M., Redding, L., & Tamashiro, W. K. (1988). Dirofilaria immitis: Biochemical and immunological characterization of the surface antigens from adult parasites. *Experimental Parasitology, 67*(2), 307-323. doi: 10.1016/0014-4894(88)90078-1

Smith, F. H. (1903). *The under dog.* New York: Charles Scribner's Sons.

Steere, A. C., Coburn, J., & Glickstein, L. (2004). The emergence of Lyme disease. *Journal of Clinical Investigation, 113*(8), 1093-1101. doi: 10.1172/JCI21681

Supakorndej, P., Lewis, R. E., McCall, J. W., Dzimianski, M. T., & Holmes, R. A. (1995). Radiographic and angiographic evaluations of ferrets experimentally infected with Dirofilaria immitis. *Veterinary Radiology Ultrasound, 36*(1), 23-29. doi: 10.1111/j.1740-8261.1995.tb00208.x

Takruri, H. H., & Dameh, M. F. (1998). Study of the nutritional value of black cumin seeds (Nigella sativaL). *Journal of the Science of Food and Agriculture, 76*(3), 404-410. doi: 10.1002/(SICI)1097-0010(199803)76:33.0.CO;2-L

Tekeoglu, I., Dogan, A., & Demiralp, L. (2006). Effects of thymoquinone (volatile oil of black cumin) on rheumatoid arthritis in rat models. *Phytotherapy Research, 20*(10), 869-871. doi: 10.1002/ptr.1964

Thippeswamy, N. B., & Naidu, K. A. (2005). Antioxidant potency of cumin varieties cumin, black cumin and bitter cumin on antioxidant systems. *European Food Research and Technology, 220*(5-6), 472-476. doi: 10.1007/s00217-004-1087-y

Venco, L., McCall, J., Guerrero, J., & Genchi, C. (2004). Efficacy of long-term monthly administration of ivermectin on the progress of naturally acquired heartworm infections in dogs. *Veterinary Parasitology, 124*(3-4), 259-268. doi: 10.1016/j.vetpar.2004.06.024

Venco, L., Mortarino, M., Carro, C., Genchi, M., Pampurini, F., & Genchi, C. (2008). Field efficacy and safety of a combination of moxidectin and imidacloprid for the prevention of feline heartworm (Dirofilaria immitis) infection. *Veterinary Parasitology, 154*(1-2), 67-70. doi: 10.1016/j.vetpar.2008.02.020

Index

A

B

C

F

G

H

I

J

L

M

N

O

P

Q

R

S

T

U

W

X

Y

Z

Made in the USA
Lexington, KY
19 September 2017